Who's Teaching Your Children?

VIVIAN TROEN & KATHERINE C. BOLES

Who's Teaching Your Children?

Why the Teacher Crisis Is Worse Than You

Think and What Can Be Done About It

YALE UNIVERSITY PRESS / NEW HAVEN & LONDON

Printed in the United States of America.

Library of Congress Cataloging-in-Publication Data
Troen, Vivian, 1940–
Who's teaching your children? : why the teacher crisis is worse than you think and what can be done about it / Vivian Troen and Katherine C. Boles.
   p.   cm.
Includes bibliographical references and index.
ISBN 0-300-09741-7 (cloth : alk. paper)
1. Elementary school teachers—United States—Social conditions. 2. Elementary school teachers—Training of—United States. 3. Educational change—United States. I. Boles, Katherine. II. Title.
LB1776.2 .T76 2002
372.11′00973—dc21   2002012966

A catalogue record for this book is available from the British Library.

The paper in this book meets the guidelines for permanence and durability of the Committee on Production Guidelines for Book Longevity of the Council on Library Resources.

10 9 8 7 6 5 4 3 2 1

To the hardest working, least appreciated, most undervalued worker in our society; linchpin of democracy and conveyor of American values and culture; conservator of our most valuable national asset; indispensable determiner of our future—the classroom teacher.

Contents

Foreword

For the layperson who wants to gain an understanding of why educational reform has advanced so little, this is the best book I have come across. I have been in and around the reform movement for more than forty years. I have written a fair amount about it. However much I hoped my books would be read by people other than educators, they were in fact the primary audience I sought to reach. If my hope for a wider audience was dashed, I am confident that a different fate awaits this book.

It reads like a novel, yet at the same time it consistently describes what everyone in the reform movement has experienced. No one until now, however, has expressed those views in such a personal, compelling, poignant, humorous, and inspiring way. In their writings, academics tend to reveal little of themselves, and they seldom divulge either the strong and conflicting emotions and opinions engendered by the attempt to spearhead change or the naïveté their mistakes reveal. The authors of this book have been and still are teachers (among other things), but that is not the half of it. They have always been reformers who have overcome obstacles, internal and external. Although Troen and Boles hope that their book will be read by educators, their primary audience is the *educated public* puzzled by, disappointed in, or simply curious about educational reform and why it is at the top of the societal agenda. *Who's Teaching Your Children?* is written to reach that public, and the authors succeed because of the kind of people they are: audacious, honest, self-confident, unafraid to own up to mistakes, articulate, persevering, and in the top 1 percent of the population for street smarts. They are thinkers, conceptualizers, and activists. And wonder of wonders, they can write! I said that the book reads like a novel, and I would be mightily surprised if readers did not agree with me. This is an "inside story": what schools are like, why teachers and students are victims, why preparatory programs perpetuate the problem, why people generally cannot be, as they should be, a force for change, because they have little idea of the inside story. As a result, the authors show, reformers fall prey to simple solutions, thus confirming Mencken's caveat that for every important problem there is a simple solution that is wrong.

The only time I have depressive tendencies is when I think about how we can improve our schools. That is when I need a dose of intellectual Prozac. That is why reading this book was such a joy. Here were two people who told the inside story of schooling with brilliance, honesty, and, most surprising, with sympathy and humor. It reminded me of my favorite American novel, which contains the inside story of American politics. Like the two authors of this book, the writer, Edwin O'Connor, was a Bostonian. I refer, of course, to *The Last Hurrah*.

We are used to hearing that war is too important to be left to the generals. Education and its reform are too important to be left to the educators, who, like generals, it must be said, will have to play a very important role. The battle for our schools, however, will be fought in the trenches. Teaching reform will never be effective unless the general public becomes aware of the crucial issues.

I find this book inspiring because of the two people whose life stories it contains: for a couple of decades—and despite differences in personality, background, religion, and family obligations—they have pursued an odyssey that is by no means finished. They have accomplished a great deal and, I predict, will accomplish more: one must hope that their ideas will percolate.

This is not to say that the authors have posed and answered all the questions; they have not, and they know it. It is only fair to note too that other books and other teachers have attempted to tell the inside story. If I am enthusiastic about *Who's Teaching Your Children?* it is not only because it tells the story more appealingly but because it gives the public a more realistic picture of the current self-defeating state of affairs.

Vivian Troen and Kitty Boles's account comes at a time when the American public needs to know the inside story. Here it is: not only a compelling analysis and convincing plan for action, but a darned good read.

Seymour B. Sarason
professor emeritus of psychology
Yale University

Acknowledgments

Over the past fifteen years we have visited dozens of schools in our quest to gain a deeper understanding of teachers and their practice. The generosity and candor of the many unnamed teachers and principals around the world, from Europe to South Africa to Australia to Japan to South America and here at home, in urban and rural schools and on Native American reservations, were overwhelming and we owe those educators our sincere gratitude. They opened their schools, their classrooms, their meetings, and sometimes their homes, and they freely shared their secrets and their stories. The teachers and principals we met all wanted us to know about both their disappointments and their triumphs, and we are honored to have learned so much from them.

We have been greatly influenced by our colleagues at the Edward Devotion School in Brookline, Massachusetts, where we both taught for more than twenty years. Our principal, Jerry Kaplan, now retired, believed in us and championed our radical ideas; today each of us has his picture on her desk. We are especially indebted to the teachers who were part of our team in the Learning/Teaching Collaborative: Janice Danielson, Jack DeLong, Andrea Doane, Nancy Frane, Mark Jacobson, Betsy Kellogg, Betsy Lake, Jim Swaim, and the late Joanne

Rostler. Gifted Brookline administrators who were also our mentors throughout this process were Patricia Ruane, Louise Thompson, Naomi Gordon, and Robert Sperber. Over the years they supported us with sound advice and steadying optimism. Our thanks go, too, to Jon Saphier, who inspired us with his philosophical outlook, to Donald Freeman of the School for International Training, who gave us help in South Africa and Japan, and to Ken Zeichner, who very early on looked at our initial draft.

We must single out two teacher interns, now our friends and accomplished classroom teachers, Francesca Stark and Rebecca Goodman, who have, among other things, given us insights into the culture of schools and taught us a great deal about the complexity and challenges of teacher induction.

Many people read and commented on our book. Seymour Sarason expressed his tremendous enthusiasm for our work from the very beginning. Knowing that he believed in our book was immensely important as we struggled through drafts and revisions. When we couldn't find a publisher, Arthur Golden took the time to do a thoughtful review of our first completed manuscript and told us it was a good initial effort, but to throw it all out and start again (as he had done many times with *Memoirs of a Geisha*). We followed his advice. Arthur also was kind enough to write down a list of useful phrases in Japanese for our introduction at Japanese schools. Karen Worth of Wheelock College, an early contributor of ideas and suggestions, taught us to think in new ways and proffered many provocative comments; her detailed responses to our manuscript resulted in substantial improvements. We are indebted to Joyce Antler, historian and chair of the American Studies Department at Brandeis University, for her expert advice and for critically important suggestions that contributed immeasurably to our work, and to Susan Moore Johnson, professor of education at Harvard University, a wonderful and attentive mentor whose interest in teachers and teaching has been inspirational to us. Author Lora Brody, our dear friend, lent her creative expertise as the book neared completion, and provided energy and support throughout. Elaine Israel and Judy McCarthy gave us frank and useful appraisals of our manuscript.

We have benefited from these valued colleagues: Marsha Levine at NCATE, for listening to our ranting in her calm, collected way and offering sage advice that helped us refine our ideas; and Bella Rosenberg, Sylvia Seidel, Joan Baratz-Snowden, and Ed Doherty for providing helpful information about current school reform efforts around the United States from a union perspective. Any discussion of teachers unions would be incomplete without a mention of our dear friend, now gone, Albert Shanker. A large man often scrunched into a small office, Al was for many years—a lifetime, really—a giant on the landscape of American education. He was instrumental in launching our collaboration and his magic wand opened many doors for us.

We are most appreciative of the help given us by Richard Murnane of the Harvard Graduate School of Education, who offered great encouragement while we were conducting our research and who introduced us to his editor, Susan Arellano at Yale University Press. It was a fortuitous introduction for, thanks in great part to Susan's efforts, Yale accepted our book for publication. We also believe ourselves fortunate to have been put into the able hands of Sarah Lawsky, our subsequent editor at Yale.

We are grateful for the extended conversations, exchanges of papers, and friendships with Roland Barth, Bob Peterkin, and Paul Reville. Stanley Sagov contributed valuable insights in the field of education for preservice and veteran physicians. David Haselkorn contributed important data gleaned from research studies on teacher recruitment.

The support of a Spencer MacArthur Grant helped us gain invaluable insight into the culture of schools, and we benefited from the wise counsel of Patricia Albjerg Graham; we also thank Mark Rigdon and John Rury for their support of our ideas.

Three librarians, enormously patient and exceptionally generous with their time and expertise, Deborah Garson, Marcella Flaherty, and Kathleen Donovan of Harvard's Gutman Library, tracked down elusive internet documents and ferreted out obscure references that assisted in the completion of our manuscript.

Barney Brawer and Molly Brawer were always there with frank comments, critical thinking, and sensitive feedback. Barney spent many hours brainstorming with us in the initial stages of the book and provided unflagging support throughout the writing process. Charlotte Brawer had faith in us, helped us financially when we were getting started, and offered thoughtful comments on our writing. We extend our thanks, too, to Adina Troen-Krasnow, Cheryl Futran, and Jonathan Troen, who were throughout this project wholly support-ive, recounting their teacher-parent experiences in some cases and providing telephone support in others; and a special note of thanks to Lisa Wesel, who kept us informed of late-breaking developments in education reform with numerous articles clipped from dozens of sources. Susan Eisenberg's moral support in our many walks around Jamaica Pond kept us going when obstacles blocked our path; for those bracing chats we are supremely grateful. And we are grateful to our friends at Egg Design Partners, Jonathan Jackson, Tim Preston, and especially Cynthia Delfino Quilici for her Trilemma Dysfunc-tion illustrations.

We owe an incalculable debt to Paul Wesel, without whom, it is fair to say, we would not have a book. It was his idea for us to write one and, at various times when the work was hardest, he urged us on and would not let us quit, listened to our ideas and gave them shape, helped organize the material, and for more than twenty years has been our strongest, most devoted ally and fan.

Prologue

Kitty, 1959:

In the sixth grade I already know I am going to be a teacher. It's not about changing the world. It's about being like Miss Whitbread, my teacher when I was in the fifth grade, and Mr. Baron, my teacher this year. Before Miss Whitbread, my teachers were older women with gray hair who stood solemnly at the front of the room angrily admonishing me (I'm left-handed) to hold my pencil "correctly," making me feel clumsy and unattractive and stupid. Miss Whitbread was different. She had red hair and drove a two-toned green-and-white Oldsmobile and reminded me of Nancy Drew, the heroine of the most wonderful books. Miss Whitbread told stories about her life— where she lived, what she liked to do—and she was Catholic, the first Catholic teacher I ever had. When the class recited the Lord's Prayer every morning (the Protestant version), Miss Whitbread, like me, stopped saying the prayer before the "for thine is the kingdom and the glory forever and ever" ending. And once in a while, out of habit, Miss Whitbread made the mistake of beginning to make the sign of the cross after she finished reciting the prayer, just the way I did. It embarrassed me when I did it, but here was this wonderful, perfect person who did the same thing. I had found a soul mate. Miss Whitbread told my parents that their daughter had a "wonderful memory." She gave me the job of counting stamp money (War Bond stamps were purchased once a week), and she put me in the top reading group. Reading *groups* were a new idea at the John Lewis Childs School in Floral Park, New York. Before that, reading lessons were given to the whole class, and the evil children who lost their place in the read-aloud lessons as the teacher went around the room with each child reading a paragraph were forced to stand for the remainder of the reading period.

When I tell my parents that I am going to be a teacher, they are pleased, in their quiet, accepting way. Everyone is satisfied with my decision. It is regularly stated that Kitty's going to be a teacher when she grows up. The perfect job for a woman, my mother says. And in the fifth grade, it seems glamorous, as well. My sixth grade teacher, Mr. Baron, is a Jewish man from Queens. He's thirty-one years old, he tells us, and he opens a whole wondrous new world, thereby clinching my decision to become a teacher. At the back of our large, messy classroom is a row of cages filled with animals, the most exciting of which is a boa constrictor. The rows we sit in are regularly rotated, and I eagerly anticipate my turn to be seated next to the boa. When I go home one afternoon and tell how I've been seated next to this creature and how I spend the day watching the snake move and stick out its tongue, the family howls at my demonstration. We study airplanes. Lift, pitch, yaw, and rudders and ailerons. We make balsa wood models, cutting the pieces carefully with X-acto knives and gluing them together with Duco cement. Mr. Baron, who plays the piano, loves musical theater, and in the winter the entire class puts on a production of *The Mikado*. To prepare for the production, Mr. Baron takes us to a Chinese restaurant, and I have my first taste of barbecued spare ribs, and my first encounter with chopsticks. I have the role of Pitti-Sing, one of the three little maids from school, and the world becomes bigger and more interesting to this shy and "introverted" girl, as one teacher calls me. Miss Whitbread and Mr. Baron give us dreams and aspirations and memories.

Forty years from now, the smell of Duco cement and Chinese food will transport me back to the sixth grade and Mr. Baron. I will keep my costume from *The Mikado,* the lovely flowered kimono with the sky-blue trim, carefully tucked away in a drawer in my bedroom. I will remember with sadness that Mr. Baron, considered weird and eccentric by the other teachers, who shunned him, died in his early fifties, disappointed and burned out. But in the sixth grade, confidence in my decision steadies my ambition—to be a teacher as beautiful and vivacious as Miss Whitbread, and as gifted and inspiring as Mr. Baron.

Vivian, 1961:

In my memory, it is late spring. Another oppressively hot and windy day in Bet Shemesh, and with the *hamsin* there is the ominous hint of an approaching dust storm. A half hour's bus ride from Jerusalem, Bet Shemesh is a small town, with a settlement of low buildings housing a number of immigrant Yemenite families. I walk through the Yemenite section on my way to the bus stop. I am twenty years old, recently married, and work part-time as the manager of an art gallery in Jerusalem while taking classes at Hebrew University—a transplanted American. I am pregnant. My life is in flux. I am preoccupied with the approaching storm, which mirrors my own ambiguities about living in this turbulent country in a time of high excitement and national struggle. Will my first child be born here? What will happen to my studies?

The dust rises and swirls through the narrow streets, past the open doorways. Barefoot children, small, shy, and curious, peek out at the stranger who walks every day through their midst, seeing them but not seeing them. And yet, I am beginning to notice something peculiar. Each day the children look different to me. It seems as if yesterday's children have been replaced with another set of children, and those were somehow different from the children of the day before. Perhaps in my pregnant state I am paying more attention to the faces of all children everywhere. Then why am I unable to recognize the children who were standing in these doorways yesterday? Is there a mystery here beyond my understanding?

I slow my steps and turn aside at the next house. I pause, then approach the little girl in a yellow dress sitting on the single front step. The little girl, whose parents speak only Arabic, is learning Hebrew in school. Well, my Hebrew is almost as good as a seven-year-old's, and with my dozen words of Arabic, we are getting along fine. I ask her why she is not in school. Her eyes, which until now have been bright and full of curiosity, turn to the ground. She is looking at her feet. She says that she is not in school because it is not her turn—not her turn to have the shoes. The school administration has decreed that children must wear shoes or they cannot come to school. Her family, and almost every Yemenite family in this settlement, I suspect, has at best one pair of shoes. The shoes are handed around from child to child, so that each child gets an equal chance to go to school, maybe once or twice a week. I am appalled at such bureaucratic stupidity. How can this happen in a free and democratic society? Where are the teachers, I wonder. Why don't they speak out? Surely, I think, if only the teachers spoke out, they could make things better for the children . . .

Introduction

You are most likely reading this book because from one perspective or another—as a parent, an educator, a taxpayer, a legislator, or a policy maker—you care about the education of children in our public schools. So do we.

We'll be blunt. Public education in America is in serious trouble. By "in trouble," we mean that the number of good classroom teachers, and therefore the quality of teaching itself, is in perilous decline and will continue to worsen. For several years we have been studying the fundamental causes for the crisis, the reason all current education reforms have not worked and will not work. This book represents the outcome of our experience and sets forth our proposed solutions to the problem.

We are two friends and colleagues who have spent a combined sixty years as classroom teachers, college educators, and education consultants to schools and school systems in the United States and other countries. We began our collaboration at the Edward Devotion School, a public elementary kindergarten through eighth grade school in Brookline, Massachusetts, where we met and began to exchange ideas on teachers and teaching.

At first, our intent was simply to improve our practice. We hooked up because we thought we were pretty good teachers who could get significantly better if we collaborated. For a kick, we started meeting regularly after school to plan lessons together, develop teaching materials, and research books and journals on the practice of teaching. The more we read, studied, and absorbed, the more deeply we examined critically the job of teaching itself.

In June 1984, Vivian and I sat in a function room of a downtown Boston hotel and wondered whether the growing strength of the women's movement was causing a downward spiral in the health of public education. Around us swirled the noise and laughter of an Edward Devotion School farewell party—an annual end-of-year event held to kiss departing teachers goodbye. These ceremonies had been held forever, and we had been going to them for several years. Lately, however, in addition to the usual gray-haired retirees, we were seeing an alarming number of young, intelligent, highly competent teachers leave Devotion, and teaching, for other jobs. This was the subject of an ongoing discussion between Vivian and me.

As we worked together, we found that our conversations increasingly turned toward the nature of teaching as a profession, and our collaboration gave us an unusual opportunity to talk about issues and ideas that teachers almost never discuss. Vivian's contention was that not only were the best teachers the ones who were leaving, but that they were being replaced with far less capable teachers, thereby degrading the overall quality of teachers, and teaching, in public schools around the country. That particular night Vivian was practically banging on the table, and while I had heard this speech before, her words on the subject were beginning to make more of an impression.

"Look around you," she said, "and see who's left and remember who's gone." Vivian held up her hand, and her fingers ticked off the score. "Marilyn Sasaki," she intoned, as if reciting a dirge of the dearly departed, "went into the insurance business. Jessica Levin—became a psychotherapist. Kate Johnson—took a job at a college. Martha Berenson—became a principal in another town. Heather Lang—went into health care. Barbara Picolo—joined a high-tech company as an executive trainer. Lisa Lunetta—got an MBA and became a consultant." She added the number of teachers who were lured into the booming eighties real estate market. A few went bust, but they never came back into teaching.

Now Vivian was using both hands, and, as she was extending her last finger, Jerry Kaplan sat down at our table and wanted to know what the game was. Jerry Kaplan, principal of the Edward Devotion School and master of ceremonies at every school event, treated these events as joyous celebrations, and we guessed that most people (besides us) felt that they were. To Jerry, these rituals in which he bade a fond farewell to each individual teacher were somewhat like rites of passage during which the participants progressed from one stage of life to another. The teachers who were leaving were *moving on,* he would say. "It's laudable for people to take advantage of *opportunities for growth,* and I encourage it." We could see that Jerry's vision of the future assumed a constant flow of good teachers into the system to replace those who were leaving. In fact, because of its reputation, Brookline continued to attract the best teachers available. But the best available were becoming not so great. The pool of excellence was drying up. The two of us were in the trenches, and we knew that the new wave of student teachers—those who were poised to enter the profession—fell several notches below those who were leaving in terms of intelligence, knowledge, capability, maturity, and talent. Vivian and I would wring our hands over the new student teachers who couldn't find Guatemala on a world map or would misspell one out of every twenty words on a blackboard. But Jerry insisted that these were anomalies, not indicators of decline.

"Then why do I feel like Jeremiah, the prophet of doom?" asked Vivian after Jerry had walked away. "If teaching is a job that's only tolerable on a short-term basis, or when other options are unavailable, what does that say about teaching and about the people who choose it as a career?"

I had no answer and went home depressed.

—Kitty

Not wanting to stay depressed forever, we began our quest to improve public education by asking ourselves whether we had the capacity to solve what was to us a mystery—why the best teachers were leaving the classroom, only to be replaced with teachers of less competence and ability. Was there something wrong with the job of teaching, that it failed to attract and keep the best?

Consider this metaphor: A swimming pool has a serious leak. You wouldn't expect that pouring more and more water into the pool would in time fix the leak, but that's precisely the approach we're taking toward the . . . teacher shortage. Everyone's noticed that the "pool" is low, and getting lower. . . . The response has been to recruit more people into teaching, using a variety of strategies . . . yet the pool keeps losing water because no one is paying attention to the leak. That is, we've misdiagnosed the problem as "recruitment" when it's really "retention." Simply put, we train teachers poorly and then treat them badly—and so they leave in droves. . . . To call for greater recruitment efforts in the face of overwhelming evidence that the system cannot *keep* people seems odd, to say the least.[1]

Looking for answers, we extended our collaboration by forming a teaching partnership, with the support and encouragement of our unusual principal, Jerry Kaplan, who gave us free rein to explore the concept of two teachers co-teaching a combined classroom. We thought other teachers might be interested in our ideas, so we wrote articles and got them published. They attracted some attention, and before long we found ourselves attending national conferences on education, serving on boards and committees, speaking before institutions, associations, and unions, delivering workshops, and taking on consulting jobs. Each of us, at separate times, took on the challenge of getting advanced degrees. We became noisy (and often bothersome) advocates of teacher empowerment. We became champions of teacher leadership, the notion that teachers could change education for the better by assuming leadership roles without leaving the classroom. In time, we built a growing network of principals, superintendents, college deans, union presidents, commissioners of education, legislators, media moilers, and leaders of reform across the broad spectrum of American education. We met and formed alliances with some of the giants of the profession (as well as some of the dwarfs), gave and shared ideas, created initiatives, and built bridges between sometimes antagonistic and adversarial constituencies.

Somewhere along the way we began to believe that part of the reason that more poorly trained teachers were coming into the classroom lay in the flawed relationship between public schools and schools of education charged with the job of preparing teachers. So we founded the Learning/Teaching Collaborative, one of the country's earliest professional development schools (school-college collaborations), a national movement that we helped pioneer. We continue to believe that professional development schools are a good idea, and they're one of the very few education reforms we enthusiastically support. Yet we have come to realize that although professional development schools are often successful in training good teachers, their efforts to improve the quality of public education are ultimately defeated.

While researching the subject of teacher preparation, we interviewed an executive at the Boston Plan for Excellence, an independent foundation whose mission it is to improve instruction in the Boston public schools. She wasn't convinced that teacher preparation had improved much in the past several years, but even that, she said, was not the most critical issue.

> It's not so much their preparation. . . . new teachers are more willing to work with colleagues. The sad part is that this willingness gets stamped out. It's what happens when they enter the school. There's no culture in the schools for it to take root. If they don't go to a school with a culture that works, they work mightily but they fail.[2]

No matter how well we prepare teachers, they will fail. "They work mightily but they fail." Even when extraordinary steps are taken to put well-prepared teachers into classrooms, still they are destined to fail. They succeed only when the culture in which they work encourages their efforts to excel. That rarely happens. Clearly, the problem of ensuring quality teaching has to do with the culture of schools, as well as with the job of teaching itself.

Why this is so, and how the culture of schools manages to defeat virtually all education reform initiatives designed to improve public education, constitute a large part of the subject of this book. In order to become an advocate for change, you have to understand what schools are all about. Be ready to have your preconceptions rearranged.

If at this point you are asking why you should bother to continue reading any further if there is no hope, let us point out that reasons exist to believe, as we do, that substantial improvement is possible. There is hope. Workable and effective solutions can be found. Things can be done to create and then maintain a community of excellence in American education. It will not be easy, but it can be done.

At the end of the book, with our description of a Millennium School, we present a clear and realistic blueprint for school reform. We believe that it could revitalize an institution which was created in the nineteenth century and is now showing clear signs of disintegration as it enters the twenty-first. First, though, we will ask the reader to accept the challenge of absorbing a bit of the background behind the problems, so that the solutions are more intelligible. In addition to telling you how things came to be the way they are, a historical perspective available to anyone who wants to do the research, we also offer an insider's view of what happens behind the scenes in public education. This dual perspective, we believe, will lead to an understanding of the mechanisms underlying the Trilemma Dysfunction —which we offer as an overview of why public education is not working very well. Then we present our solution to the problem, in the form of a new model for public elementary school education. Here is how the book is structured:

Chapter 1 explores the reasons behind the single most critical problem in public education, the chronic shortage of good teachers. We present a diagram of public education's perpetual cycle of dysfunction—the Trilemma Dysfunction, as we call it—and label its components to aid the reader in gaining an understanding of the three major areas being addressed (badly) by education reform.

Chapter 2 presents a brief history of teaching in America, from the one-room school house to the classrooms of today, in order to explain the structure and organization of schools, the feminization of teaching, and the impact of those developments on teaching and school culture. Here, also, is where we examine the first component of the Trilemma Dysfunction: the qualifications of those who choose to go into teaching.

Chapter 3 exposes the weaknesses of teacher preparation—the second component of the Trilemma Dysfunction—and reveals how inadequate teacher training and lack of follow-up professional development affect the quality of classroom teaching.

Chapter 4 describes the third component of the Trilemma Dysfunction—the professional work life of the teacher—and shows how the culture of schools and schooling defeats good teachers, obstructs education reform, and makes teaching an undesirable job for well-qualified people who have other choices.

Chapter 5 identifies the most popular of today's education reforms and analyzes why each of them fails to achieve its purpose. The chapter also describes the role of the unions in education reform, their obstructionist past and their transitional present, and offers an optimistic view of their future.

Chapter 6 proposes our solution to the dysfunctions of public education in the form of what we call a Millennium School. We describe the components and features of a Millennium School, how it is structured, staffed, and operated; and we present a fictional day in the life of a "typical" Millennium School to show the reader how the whole thing works.

For the two of us, writing this book together presented a dilemma. The authors are two people with three voices: I, I, and we. We have tried to make this dilemma as easy as possible on the reader by identifying who is doing the talking when it is not both of us (as in the anecdotes above). Therefore, you can assume that when we say "we" it means both of us, except at those times when "we" means all of us in this country or in this society, or us as human beings. We leave it to the reader, whose intelligence we trust, to sort it out.

There are other voices in this book, too, and we identify them where we can. Some people's names are real, and some are not. Sometimes people say or do things they would rather not be associated with in print, and we have tried to be careful about that.

One final declaration is necessary. We both love teaching, and have always loved it. We have devoted our professional lives to it and still do. Now, after a combined six decades of it, we do less teaching than we used to, but our passion for the excitement of the classroom remains undiminished.

We only wish that excellent teaching were encouraged, supported, and rewarded in every classroom in America. It is our dream that someday it may be so.

Let us be clear about this: good teachers are not extinct. We have visited a great many schools in this country and are confident that every school in the United States has at least one excellent teacher, sometimes two. But a war cannot be won with one or two good soldiers in every division, and excellence in education cannot be achieved with one or two good teachers per school.

This book is about how to make sure that good teachers—and good teaching—are the norm, and not the exception.

1 Your Children Aren't Getting the Teachers They Deserve

I have never let my schooling interfere with my education.
—Mark Twain

According to a recent Lou Harris poll, nearly 90 percent of Americans believe that putting a well-qualified teacher in every public school classroom is the best way to raise student achievement. They also believe that the quality of the current teaching force does not measure up to what children need and what the nation's educational goals demand. Fewer than a quarter believe that their local school district always hires fully qualified teachers. Fewer than a third believe that their state's current teacher licensing requirements ensure that teachers really know how to teach. Fewer than a fifth say that teachers in their own community are highly qualified. Seventy-eight percent say that the problem of incompetent teachers is widespread. Unequivocally, Americans state that the highest priority of education reform should be to *fix teaching first*.[1]

The Big Questions

We believe that the American public is smarter about education reform than most of the people who are put in charge of it.

A majority of American parents secretly suspect, or openly acknowledge, that too many of the teachers who are teaching their children are just not as good as the teachers they had when they themselves were in school. Why is it, they wonder, that their children aren't learning math or reading at grade level, and that teachers are failing to take responsibility for their lack of success in teaching the fundamentals? Why is it, after all the time, energy, money, and brainpower devoted to improving public education, that nothing seems to have any substantial or lasting effect? Why is it, after all is said and done, that the quality of classroom teaching seems to get worse year after year?

Parents' suspicions and concerns are well founded.

My daughter will be kindergarten age in the fall, so I started to scope out the schools in my area. There aren't a lot of choices, so I thought I'd begin with a visit to the local elementary school. I went to public schools, my husband went to public schools, my mother and grandmother were public school teachers, and I thought, given a choice, I'd rather have my kids in the public schools. We're paying the taxes. My visit was an eye-opener, and a shock I wasn't prepared for. The class was being taught by a young, low-energy woman who seemed most of the time to be mentally somewhere else. The kids weren't excited. She wasn't excited. The kids sat in desultory circles, sang desultory songs, accomplished desultory tasks while the teacher appeared to be sleepwalking. Okay, I thought, maybe she's just having a bad day. When they sat down to draw, though, was where I went over the edge. "Take out your green crayons," she said, "you won't need any other colors, because we're going to be drawing frogs, and frogs are green." Oh my God, I thought. Not only does this teacher not want any child to have any free expression, she doesn't even know that there are such things as orange

frogs and blue frogs and purple frogs! Get me outta here! I enrolled my girl in a private school. It's a stretch financially, but I wouldn't subject my daughter to that environment. I don't care what it takes.
—Parent, Bowdoinham, Maine

In our opinion, classroom teaching competency is lower now than it has been since the era of the one-room schoolhouse. Nationally, public education is in a state of disarray. The 1999 Third International Mathematics and Science Study-Repeat (TIMSS-R), showed U.S. eighth graders ranking seventeenth among the thirty-eight countries that participated in the study.[2] Commenting on that study, a writer for the journal *Education Week* observed, "If the United States ranked seventeenth in the world in Olympic medals, it would be a national embarrassment. . . . Why can't the same be true of education?"[3] Desperate parents are pulling their children out of public schools and looking for alternatives. Private school admissions and homeschooling are on the rise. Educators and policy makers continue to propose one short-sighted and ineffective solution after another. *Education reform* is a term on everyone's lips, but it is a phrase without meaning unless the underlying causes of declining teacher quality are being addressed. And they aren't.

It is time to ask why the shortage of qualified teachers is so acute. In the next decade we will need to hire more than 2.2 million new teachers, and nobody knows where we are going to find them.[4] To compound the problem, the best teachers are leaving America's classrooms at an accelerating rate. As experienced teachers retire or leave for better career opportunities elsewhere, they are being replaced with underqualified, poorly trained novices with little or no experience who, when they enter the classroom, receive inadequate supervision and even less support. One in five will leave within the first three years.[5] The quality of teaching therefore continues to decline nationwide. The problem is most critical in inner-city schools, but even the wealthiest school districts are not immune. There are simply not enough good teachers to go around. In the United States, a technologically advanced democracy dependent on education to produce an informed electorate, 30 percent of novice teachers entering the classroom scored in the bottom quartile on their college entrance exams.[6]

Teaching—as it *should* be practiced—requires years of training, immense technical knowledge, and intellectual rigor. But there is a gap between how teaching ought to be practiced and how it is practiced in today's classrooms. Within that gap lie the seeds of failure for the American system of public education.

Quality education begins with quality teaching, but teaching is a job that fewer and fewer people of quality want to do. Why are fewer good people attracted to teaching? Why are they so poorly trained? Why do so many good people leave?

The Big Picture

To answer those questions, let's begin by taking a look at the late 1970s. At that time President Jimmy Carter, fearing that the economy was in serious trouble, spoke of a "national malaise." Japan was surpassing the United States in industrial efficiency; American industry was in a state of disrepair. Reindustrialization was clearly necessary. Factories were crumbling, and the tried and true American systems—the assembly line and a hierarchical business structure—were seen as contributing to deterioration and obsolescence. Productivity was down. The nation's infrastructure—roads and bridges, harbors, railroads, sewer systems—was showing dramatic signs of decay. Traditional family life was in disarray, with the divorce rate at an all-time high, and the number of Americans who had slipped below the poverty line, despite the Great Society's war on poverty, seemed to be increasing. Women were entering the workforce in ever larger numbers, but now it took two medium incomes to sustain a family in the middle class instead of the single income that had been sufficient in the post–World War II years.

Unemployment was soaring, and the high school dropout rate, though lower than in the 1950s, seemed more acute because fewer jobs were available. In the 1950s a 50 percent high school dropout rate was acceptable: there was plenty of work. Members of the "blue-collar aristocracy" earned high salaries, and the standard of living in the United States during the 1950s was the envy of the world.

By the 1970s though, the booming Japanese economy was eating away at America's economic lead, and its self-confidence. Japan had new factories, new industrial methods, new products—and its educational system provided industry with technologically savvy graduates. The Cold War was waning, but a new war was looming, a war of international corporate competition, and it did not look as if the United States would win. A crisis was in the making.

In the search for solutions, the spotlight was turned on American education, and it was found wanting. Already, SAT verbal scores had dropped more than fifty points between 1963 and 1980 (among students who are today's parents and who protest that their children aren't even getting teachers as good as theirs). Although more students remained in high school than in the 1950s, they were far less able on graduation to meet the demands of the changing workplace. Industry leaders complained that the students they hired were not well educated and did not have the skills necessary to help boost American productivity and compete in the global economy.[7]

One reaction to the problems in public education was to turn away from the public schools and look to private schools for solutions. In the late 1970s a battle took place in Congress over tuition tax credits that would enable parents to send their children to parochial and private schools. The House of Representatives passed legislation supporting the use of tax vouchers, but the Democratic Senate under

President Carter (narrowly) defeated it. Albert Shanker, president of the American Federation of Teachers, called this brush with disaster the wake-up call for America.[8] Unless the education establishment rose to the challenge, he warned, the days of public education were numbered. Growing concern over the politics and processes of public education also gave birth to the movement which was to become known as homeschooling.

With the election of Ronald Reagan to the presidency in 1980, the debate gained in intensity. Reagan (who as governor of California had been instrumental in disemboweling one of the country's finest education systems) directed his secretary of education, T. H. Bell, to create the National Commission on Excellence in Education. Its mission was to examine the quality of education in the United States and deliver a report to the country within eighteen months.

Among other things, the commission was charged with assessing the quality of teaching and learning in U.S. schools, comparing American schools with those of other nations, and identifying the problems that needed to be overcome in order for America to achieve educational excellence.

The commission's thirty-six-page report, *A Nation at Risk: The Imperative for Educational Reform,* was released in April 1983. It was a bombshell. The report stated that American education as a system was "being eroded by a rising tide of mediocrity." Presenting statistic after statistic, *A Nation at Risk* laid bare the failings and inadequacies of American education at virtually every level and in chilling detail. Some 13 percent of all seventeen-year-olds in the United States were found to be functionally illiterate.[9] International comparisons of student achievement revealed that on nineteen academic tests American students never finished first or second and, in comparison with other industrialized nations, came in last seven times. The average achievement of American high school students on most standardized tests had fallen below the levels as tested twenty-six years previously, at the time Sputnik was launched. The report revealed manifold failures: in the quality of school curricula, in school year scheduling and the use of school time, in low expectations of student achievement, and in the recruitment, training, qualification, pay, and working conditions of the nation's teachers. In summarizing its findings regarding teaching, the commission reported "that not enough of the academically able students are being attracted to teaching; that teacher preparation programs need substantial improvement; that the professional life of teachers is on the whole unacceptable; and that a serious shortage of teachers exists in key fields."[10]

Presented under the auspices of a popular president who had elected to take on the education establishment, *A Nation at Risk* garnered national, media-fueled attention. The damning assessment of the ill health of America's schools was followed by a flurry of reports and numerous state reform initiatives. These initiatives called for the implementation of new rules and regulations to improve schools significantly.

The first states to rise to the challenge were in the South. Southern states, which had a legacy of poor education systems, were experiencing their greatest population growth and economic resurgence since the end of the Civil War. Lured by cheap labor, the low cost of real estate, and attractive tax breaks, industries were moving south. Corporate recruiters, however, were dismayed by the low skills of Southern workers. Southern governors, realizing that businesses would more readily relocate to areas with an educated workforce, determined that investing in education would be the key to sustaining the new economic growth.

Texas was first. Under the leadership of Mark White, an education-minded governor who had a major involvement in the business community, Texas established an education commission that decided on massive regulatory changes and poured large sums of money into education.[11] In return, the state demanded that teachers be tested.

A parallel development took place in Tennessee. Under Governor Lamar Alexander, a "better schools program" was created that established a so-called career ladder for teachers, which consisted mostly of increased pay for greater classroom experience and included teacher testing as well.[12] Kentucky reformed its entire funding structure for education and significantly increased its spending on school improvement.[13] Suddenly, it seemed, the country was paying attention to education.

A Nation At Risk had started the ball rolling, and soon there would be other, equally damning studies and reports on the state of American education. The gauntlet had been flung down, creating both a new agenda for educators and policy makers and a weapon for would-be reformers.

Publication of *A Nation At Risk* attracted attention to the broad range of problems in the nation's schools, from high dropout rates to low reading comprehension. In reaction, a blizzard of legislative proposals called for periodic standardized testing, merit pay programs, and more strenuous graduation requirements. Those solutions, which were initiated from above but never embraced at the classroom level, failed to realize their desired goal. In spite of all efforts, student achievement remained disappointingly low.

There was a general sense of stagnation in America's schools, the gnawing fear that we were going to be left behind in the global economy unless strong measures were taken to solve "the problems of education," however those were defined. Politicians and policy makers and heads of educational institutions, however, were feeling the pressure to do *something*.

More than twenty years later, after hundreds of reports, dozens of initiatives, and many billions of dollars (education in the United States is a $600-billion-a-year industry), little has been accomplished in the way of true education reform. And that awful, nagging feeling of having to do *something* has not abated. If anything, it has intensified. What do the pollsters and the politicians discover when they take the pulse and measure the mood of the American electorate? Listed at the top of America's most urgent concerns is Education, with a capital E. Through peace and war, economic boom and bust, there is no more enduring topic. The public's painful recognition that America's education system is in danger of failing to serve the majority of our children will not fade away—unlike other subjects that vie briefly for attention until the next wave of media frenzy has crested and gone.

The only thing that has changed is that the students of twenty years ago, those who were at that time swimming in "the rising tide of mediocrity," are today's teachers. Whoa! Now there's a scary thought, because the core message of *A Nation At Risk,* in three simple sentences, is a shocking revelation of why public education is in trouble:

- Not enough academically able students are being attracted to teaching.
- Teacher preparation programs need substantial improvement.
- The professional life of teachers is on the whole unacceptable.

A problem comprising two equally unpalatable components is a dilemma. When the number of components is three, we figure, you have a *trilemma.* Our thesis is that the above-listed three critical components of the institution we call public education form a perfect, self-perpetuating cycle of dysfunction. We call this the Trilemma Dysfunction (see page 22).

Once we step back and look at the big picture, we can more easily appreciate why the bits and pieces of education reform, like Band-Aids applied to one scratch when the body has traumatic wounds all over, have failed to cure the ills of public education. To inflict another analogy on the reader, a small application of education reform—even if it costs millions—is like a pebble thrown into a river. After causing

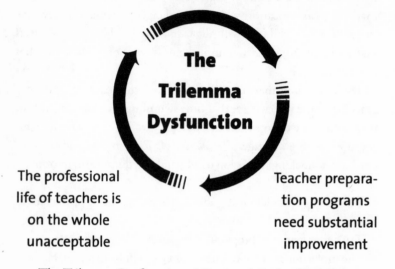

Not enough
academically able
students are being
drawn to teaching

The
Trilemma
Dysfunction

The professional
life of teachers is
on the whole
unacceptable

Teacher prepara-
tion programs
need substantial
improvement

The Trilemma Dysfunction: A Perpetual Cycle of Pathology

a small ripple, it quickly disappears and fails to change the river's course.

In this book we examine the major components of the Trilemma Dysfunction, along with their several ancillaries. We reveal why too few academically gifted students are attracted to teaching, how teacher preparation programs ill equip novice teachers for success in the classroom, and why the work life of classroom teachers is so miserable that it discourages the best of them and makes the job of teaching unattractive to people who might otherwise want to become teachers, thereby perpetuating the cycle of dysfunction.

In conclusion we present a blueprint for serious and comprehensive education reform. We believe that it would, if instituted, go further than any proposed so far toward breaking the cycle of dysfunction that continues to degrade the quality of public education.

**Not enough
academically able
students are being
drawn to teaching**

The professional
life of teachers is
on the whole
unacceptable

Teacher prepara-
tion programs
need substantial
improvement

Too Few Good Candidates Want to Become Teachers

2 How Teaching Got to Be This Way

In a completely rational society, the best of us would aspire to be teachers and the rest of us would have to settle for something less, because passing civilization along from one generation to the next ought to be the highest honor and responsibility anyone could have. —Lee Iacocca

---

The first settlers of our country, in the Northeast, were literate. The colonies were populated by English-speaking Protestants. Literacy was important to them, for Bible study was a cornerstone of their faith. Although this commitment to the value of literacy was at first religious, it soon worked its way into the fabric of American culture, as rapidly emerging economic and social concerns became a powerful influence in the establishment of schools.

Since most eighteenth-century communities were small—no larger than 2,500 people—the first schools were rural one-room schoolhouses. They remained the model for how public education was administered until the middle of the nineteenth century.[1]

The American Teacher

Most of us have a romanticized picture of the early one-room school, one in which a motley group of children of varying ages, warmed by a pot-bellied stove, share a small supply of textbooks and materials, under the eye of a stern but benevolent schoolmaster who strictly applies the basic rules of reading, writing, and arithmetic. In fact, the early one-room schoolhouses were bleak, primitive buildings—spare, filthy, badly heated, and often administered by ne'er-do-well young males who were meagerly paid, sometimes sadistic, and answerable to a stingy and watchful community. These schoolmasters, rarely well educated themselves, were often hardly better off than their pupils. Books and materials were donated by members of the community, when they were available, and parents contributed wood for the stove as their payment for lessons.

Some teachers, part-time divinity students, were better qualified than most. Some were transients wending their way from community to community, stopping for a period of a year or two before their incompetencies were uncovered and they were forced to move on. There were no requirements for being a schoolmaster, only the ability to read and write and the physical strength or personal charm to manage even the largest intransigent farm boy. Physical punishment was regularly employed as a method of keeping discipline. The "curriculum" was whatever the local community said it wanted its children to learn. Yet it must be remembered that, for all its deficiencies, the one-room schoolhouse did manage to bring some measure of literacy to a broad range of citizens for whom education had previously been inaccessible. It was the first and necessary step in a noble vision of democracy that depended on universal education, a concept untested anywhere else in the world.

As America rushed headlong into the nineteenth century, two factors combined to change the nature of the rural one-room schoolhouse: increasing industrialization and rapid population growth. In 1800 the population of New York City was 60,000. By 1900 it had exploded to reach 1 million. In a single year, 1847, Boston's population of 114,000 expanded by 37,000 Irish immigrants. Nationwide, from 1820 to 1860 the number of people living in urban settlements grew from just under 700,000 to more than 6 million.[2]

It soon became painfully clear that more schools and a better-educated workforce of teachers were needed quickly. A jumble of schools employing methods barely adequate to teach literacy to farm children was not going to provide the workers needed for an industrialized nation. Awareness was growing, too, that some standards of efficiency and bureaucratization would have to be imposed if schools were to emulate what education reformers saw and liked, in the new technologies and organizations taking shape around them in the factories, railroads, and businesses of the day.

Rather than a coherent system, public education in the teeming cities consisted of a miscellaneous collection of one-room schoolhouses, each with one teacher responsible for teaching an ungraded class, pretty much as it had been since the previous century. Yet such visionary reformers as Horace Mann, Massachusetts secretary of education, faced considerable resistance in their efforts to impose substantial improvements on the prevailing chaos. Mann vigorously championed the sort of school organization, with graded classes and a well-articulated curriculum, that he had investigated and admired in Prussia, but his initial efforts succeeded only in earning him the enmity of those whose self-interest lay in preserving the status quo. It fell to John D. Philbrick, a noted educator of his time, to convince the Boston school board to follow Mann's model by creating a four-story school building for 700 students and twelve *graded* classrooms, each with its own teacher and fifty-six students. Each student would have his own desk, and the school was to be administered by a principal. Quincy School opened in Boston in 1848, initiating the model for elementary schools—called by many the egg-crate school—that survives to this day. A survey of forty-five cities conducted by the U.S. commissioner of education only twenty-two years later showed that Horace Mann's vision of the graded elementary school had become the national norm.[3]

As the growing number of shops and factories absorbed men as workers, mechanization made farm life easier for women, freeing them to seek work outside the farm. A great many women went into the factories and mills, but the better educated were able to become teachers. In Massachusetts, the first state to promote the employment of women as teachers, women outnumbered men two to one in 1842. In 1870, 59 percent of the teachers in the United State were women, a figure that grew to 70 percent in 1900 and 86 percent in 1920. In the cities, the proportions were greater. In fourteen representative cities, 90 percent of the schoolteachers were women in 1885 (a ratio that remains roughly the same in elementary schools today).[4]

The "feminization" of teaching was perfectly suited to the country's social, economic, and political needs. Women had been the traditional child-care providers, guiding their own children's educational and social development while deferring to the judgment of men, who made all the larger decisions. Women were more subservient than men and complained less about the dreadful classroom conditions of that period, an important factor in a school hierarchy under the control of male principals, superintendents, and school commissioners. And women worked for less money. In 1870, the average weekly pay of a woman elementary school teacher was $12; for men it was $35. In New York, some school districts found that they could, with the state subsidy of half a teacher's salary, employ a woman to teach full-time and thus not have to bear any of the costs themselves.[5]

At the same time, outspoken women such as Catherine Beecher became advocates for what they believed to be the civilizing influence of women in the burgeoning schools of the frontier West, as well as in the classrooms filling with immigrant children in the East. She and others championed the cause of women going into teaching rather than into factory work. Inside classrooms they could play a more important role in instituting cultural changes that would enhance the status of women in the society opening up to them outside the home. They could also stave off the threat (as she saw it) to American democracy posed by the coming generations of undereducated lower-class people.

So women were encouraged to enter the teaching profession by both powerful men and socially progressive women. Paradoxically, when economic production was transferred from the household to the factory, the status of women in society deteriorated instead of improving. Women had played a large and obvious role in the household prior to industrialization, and society acknowledged this contribution by granting women more personal autonomy in the eighteenth century, when they worked on the farms, than they were to experience in the nineteenth working in factories.

> The employment of teaching children is regarded as the most wearying drudgery, and few resort to it except from necessity; and one very reasonable cause of this aversion is the utter neglect of any arrangements of preparing teachers for the arduous and difficult profession. . . . As if a girl were sent into a splendid orchestra, all ignorant and unskillful and then required to draw a melody from each instrument and then to combine the whole into faultless harmony. . . . Look now into this small school-room where are assembled a collection of children, with a teacher unskilled in her art. What noise and disorder!—what indolence and discontent, and misrule! The children hate school and all that belongs to it, and the teacher regards the children as little more than incarnate imps![6]

Teacher training academies were founded in the early nineteenth century, the "normal schools" dedicated to providing young women with an education appropriate for teaching the young. Teaching was the only job with any intellectual basis that was acceptable and open to women. It was also satisfying on many levels, providing a measure of status and independence and a minimal living wage. It was meant to be a short-term career, between young womanhood and marriage, and many state laws mandated that a woman leave teaching once she married. Should a woman decide she preferred a career over marriage and stay in teaching, she became an "old maid schoolteacher."

From the end of the nineteenth century to the middle of the twentieth, public education became institutionalized and its infrastructure firmly entrenched. Teachers' colleges were established to offer training in pedagogy (methods and practice—the *how* of teaching, as opposed to academic content, the *what* of teaching).

Uniform curricula and standardized tests were put into place. School boards, which were committees of business and professional elites, were modeled after corporate boards of directors. The power to administer school systems was placed in the hands of professionally trained school superintendents (a term borrowed from the railroads, which were considered to represent the acme of efficient industrial organization). Compulsory attendance was mandated by law, as was certification of both teachers and the various educational functionaries and specialists spawned by the swelling school bureaucracies. Unions had a powerful effect on reforming the prevalent inequities in pay and the oppressive working conditions.

Still, since the founding of the first graded school building more than 150 years ago, one component of public education has remained essentially the same. Today, in almost every classroom in America, one teacher can be found, teaching a single class of children, surrounded by four walls and isolated from the other teachers in her eggcrate school, very much like her predecessors in 1848.

It might surprise the reader to discover that this essentially American model of teaching has been replicated the world over. The two of us have investigated schools, teachers, teacher preparation programs, school cultures, and education systems in Europe, Asia, Africa, and the Middle East. In every classroom from the small wooden shack in a rural South African village to the multi-level steel and concrete building in downtown Tokyo, the paradigm of teaching is virtually identical. It's a world of cloned Norman Rockwell–like classrooms out there.

A few years ago my husband and I joined a rafting expedition on the Upper Yangtze River, in a remote region of south central China (formerly Tibet). Partway down the river, we went for a sightseeing walk in a small city, a bustling trade crossroads with a marvelously multicultural population (minus Caucasians). We were strolling up the main street when toward us came a group of about twenty schoolchildren, just released from school and all dressed up smartly in their colorful school clothes. It could have been a scene from any American town, for the kids were all wearing the logo-emblazoned caps, shirts, shoes, and schoolbags familiar on any street in the United States. Nike backpacks, Chicago Bulls and Yankees caps, Adidas and Reebok sneakers, Mickey Mouse T-shirts. When they saw us (perhaps the first Caucasians they had ever seen in person), they broke into excited smiles and shouted a chorus of hellos in English. We replied with a hearty *Ni Hao!*, much to the amusement of the children, who giggled with glee at our peculiar accent. Further up the street we arrived at the entrance of the school, where we introduced ourselves to the "English Teacher," who had instructed these same children on how to say hello in English. Sadly, his English was almost as deficient as our Chinese (a vocabulary of about fifteen words), but I was able to understand from him how lessons are taught in his elementary school of about five hundred students. We peeked into an empty classroom and stared in wonder. At the front of the class, a desk. On the wall behind the teacher's desk, a blackboard. Above the blackboard, instead of an American flag, the red flag of China; beside the flag, instead of a picture of George Washington, a picture of Mao Tse-tung. On the side and back walls, examples of student work hung with tacks and tape. Wooden chairs and tables. Books and notepads, pencils. The smell of detergent and chalk dust. It was reminiscent of just about every classroom I'd ever seen, and a startling reminder of how far and wide has been the influence, for better and worse, of that nineteenth-century Massachusetts educator, Horace Mann.

—Vivian

Most illuminating for us, as we continue to study schools all over the United States and around the world, is that no matter what the local culture—whether Middle Eastern, European, Asian, African, North or South American—the culture of schools and the culture of teaching remain remarkably similar. The nearly cookie-cutter replication of the Horace Mann model—an egg-crate school where teaching is performed alone and behind closed doors, mostly by women, each of whom is considered the "equal" of any other teacher in the school—defines a culture that is powerful and pervasive. It is a culture that defines the job of teaching, the character of schools, and the failure of school reform.

Who Chooses to Become a Teacher?

We would hazard a guess that if we took a poll among the readers of this book we would find that most people have at least one time in their lives been profoundly affected by an influential teacher. The testimony of famous and successful people who attest to the difference a single teacher has made in their lives is not just hyperbole. Our experience with teachers and students confirms what most people believe—that in the main, teachers are dedicated, hard-working people who are drawn to their vocation through a sense of high purpose and social conscience. They genuinely like children and want to help them to achieve success.

Concerns about the quality of classroom teachers have caused massive amounts of money and time to be spent gathering research data to test the suspicion that teachers today just don't have the academic credentials of their predecessors. A typical study is one conducted by the Commonwealth of Pennsylvania. Commenting on the study's findings, the state secretary of education reported:

> We found a system with limited assurances of competence and quality. . . . Few teacher-education programs had meaningful admission standards. Most undergraduate programs, at best, required prospective students to have a 2.5 grade point average (C+) prior to majoring in education. . . . Moreover, that requirement could be fulfilled with the easiest classes.[7]

In 1964, Title VII of the Civil Rights Act barred employment discrimination by private employers, employment agencies, and unions on the basis of race, sex, and other grounds. The Equal Employment Opportunity Commission (EEOC) was established to investigate complaints and enforce penalties. In 1973, the Civil Service Commission eliminated the height and weight requirements that had been used to discriminate against women applying for police, park service, and fire fighting jobs. The Office of Federal Contract Compliance issued guidelines prohibiting sex discrimination in employment by any federal contractor and requiring affirmative action to correct existing imbalances. The U.S. military eliminated its women-only branches, thereby opening the way for gender integration of the armed forces. The Supreme Court's affirmation of the EEOC ruling against sex-segregated help-wanted ads in newspapers allowed women to apply for jobs previously restricted to men and offering better pay and advancement opportunities.

The result: women had significantly broader career opportunities than ever before.

As more jobs offered better pay, better status and prestige, greater intellectual stimulation, and opportunities for advancement, fewer women chose to go into teaching. As more and more experienced teachers retired or left for better career opportunities elsewhere, they were replaced with less qualified, less well trained novices who, when they entered the classroom, struggled alone, without supervision or support. Thus, the quality of teaching continued to decline almost unnoticed nationwide.

I was attending a forum given at the Harvard Graduate School of Education, and a bunch of people were gravitating toward the dinner table. Ted Sizer (former dean of the graduate school and founder of the Coalition for Essential Schools) was standing next to me. We were talking about the national shortage of good teachers and Ted said, in jest but to the point, "We could solve the teacher quality problem over-

night. All we'd have to do is take away all opportunities for women to have other jobs."
—Vivian

When teaching was one of the few career choices open to educated women and members of minorities, the quality of those entering the profession was demonstrably higher than it is today. With more options available, fewer of the best candidates are choosing to become teachers—especially those with high scores in math and science.

An Educational Testing Service study revealed that high school seniors who say they intend to become teachers score near the bottom of the SAT college entrance exam. A correlation made between SAT scores and test takers' intended professions shows teaching hopefuls fourth from the bottom out of twenty vocations. This is among college-bound students who voice their *intention* to become teachers. What about the academic performance of those who actually graduate from college and are headed for a master's degree program in education? On the Graduate Record Examinations taken by candidates for graduate school, those who were headed for the education schools scored at the *bottom* of the eight graded fields—business, engineering, health sciences, humanities, life sciences, social sciences, physical sciences, and education.[8] It must also be noted that not only young college seniors but likewise veteran certified teachers looking to obtain a master's degree take the GREs, and their scores are included in this group as well.

An American master's degree in education is probably the least challenging graduate program on the planet, which may account for the fact that about half of those who do get their master's of education never go into teaching. Many simply look upon it as a quick and easy (if not cheap) way to get an advanced degree.

Teaching is, or ought to be, a difficult and complex endeavor. Its successful practice demands a rare combination of human skills and technical knowledge required in few other professions. When one considers what is expected of a teacher in terms of end results—the preservation and improvement of our culture and civilization—teaching is perhaps *the* most important job in a democratic society. Asked which profession offers the most benefit to society, 62 percent of Americans named teaching, whereas only 22 percent mentioned medicine.[9] Yet from promulgators of national education policy to professors of education to classroom teachers themselves, very few people think that teaching school is an intellectual activity.

Even the Maryland State Department of Education can't help itself. "What is your perfect vision of a school classroom? Does it involve a caring, dedicated teacher?"[10] The introduction to its forty-four-page booklet describing to parents its vision of public school education never once mentions standards for teacher competence. The Department of Education seems uninterested in forming a vision that includes well-educated, highly skilled, professionally proficient teachers.

The Maryland State Department of Education is not alone. The stereotypical picture of teachers is one of *caring* individuals whose primary tasks are to keep order in the classroom, teach the 3Rs, collect lunch money, supervise recess, and, in some schools, clean tables in the cafeteria. Teachers are often treated as semiskilled workers—glorified babysitters and high-level clerks—no matter what their competence or years of experience.

In many ways, teachers are both the perpetrators and the victims of this unfortunate situation, for theirs is but one aspect of the Trilemma Dysfunction cycle—underqualified candidates who enlist to be poorly trained in order to perform a low-status job.

Not enough
academically able
students are being
drawn to teaching

The professional
life of teachers is
on the whole
unacceptable

Teacher prepara-
tion programs
need substantial
improvement

Teachers Receive Inadequate Preparation

3 Teacher Training: How Bad Is It?

Where mediocrity is the norm, it is not long before mediocrity becomes the ideal.—A. N. Wilson

Not every potential teacher comes from the lower ranks of academic achievers. We've met many a bright young woman and man, and not only from Columbia or Stanford or Wellesley, who is intelligent, energetic, and passionate about becoming a classroom teacher. The research, however, confirms what our experience has shown: the average teacher candidate is . . . well, average. In itself, academic averageness should not present an insurmountable obstacle to becoming a great teacher.

Into the Leaky Pipeline

If, for example, the teacher preparation program into which the candidate is admitted were to compensate for academic insufficiency through academic rigor supplemented by excellent teacher preparation, that would be a first step. If, when the candidate graduated, he or she were to be subjected to a rigid screening process that eliminated the less able and passed only well-qualified teachers into the classroom, that would be a good second step. Then, if that well-prepared and fully qualified novice, once in the classroom, were to be inducted into a profession in which ongoing learning, growth, and development were part of the culture, that would be the ideal. Then, and only then, would we have the assurance that we were putting the highest-quality teachers into the classroom.

That never happens. Not in preparation, not in certification, and not in professional development.[1]

Teachers Receive Poor Preparation

The subject of teacher education has been fraught with thorny issues since before the American Revolution. In 1750, Benjamin Franklin said that the country was "suffering at present very much for want of good schoolmasters." He proposed a teacher training academy to rectify the situation.[2]

In the 1800s, education reformer Horace Mann visited Prussia and returned to the United States not only with the idea of the graded school but also with the model of the normal school for teacher training. The term *normal school* was adopted from the French *école normale* (model school). Based on the idea that teachers required a type of preparation somehow different from a classical education, the normal school concentrated on building teaching skill and separated itself from education in the liberal arts. Early on, this outlook set the stage for normal school students, who for the most part had less than a high school education, to remain deficient in the mastery of common elementary subjects. Yet the model continued to be the main source of the nation's teachers for more than a hundred years.

Departments of education attached to universities began to appear in the second half of the nineteenth century. By the beginning of the twentieth century both the normal school and the university departments of education had gained a secure place in the educational picture, and both were competing for the same candidates. At the

university level, teacher educators, hoping to raise the academic status of teacher education—and theirs as well, wanted to legitimize it as
an applied science. (The movement to elevate teaching to the status
of a profession roughly parallels the efforts of those in law and medicine to do the same.)

Normal school proponents resented the rise of university departments of education because they believed that the training of teachers
was best accomplished at the normal school, and they also took it as
an incursion onto territory that had formerly been theirs alone. They
complained that when teacher training was conducted at the college
or university, the teacher training department was considered an
appendage: it lacked the single-minded support, the overarching professional spirit, and the unity needed for successful teacher education. These were not idle concerns.

What ultimately defeated all attempts made by teacher educators
on both sides of the fence to improve the training and standards for
teacher education was the sudden and overwhelming growth in
school enrollments following World War II. From 1950 to 1960 en-
rollment in elementary and secondary schools grew more than in the
entire preceding half century—13.3 million in ten years as compared
with 11.7 million in fifty years. At roughly the same time, the number
of teachers nearly doubled—from just over a million to nearly two
million—and still couldn't keep pace with enrollments. Since then,
the supply-versus-demand dilemma has continued to worsen.[3]

It is our contention that the overall quality of teacher preparation
is at a historic low and shows no prospects for improvement any time
soon. The general quality of teachers entering the classroom is kept
low by the complicity of the two major agencies in the supply chain—
those programs and institutions charged with the training of teachers, and those at the state and local levels charged with creating and
upholding the standards for admittance into the classroom. Both are
derelict in their responsibilities to the public.

As the pool of available candidates exhibits ever lower academic achievement, entrance requirements to schools of education slide lower to accommodate the market. No college or university could stay in business for long if its classrooms were kept 75 percent empty. Maintaining high standards would result in fewer enrollments. Therefore, institutions that are engaged in maintaining teacher training programs become profit-driven organizations with weakened standards for students, curricula, and facilities. As with airlines and restaurants, their continued economic health depends on putting bodies in seats. And you don't put bodies in seats—and keep them there—if you're too tough on your customers.

> When I first came to Wheelock, the grades were pass/fail, giving the professors some leeway in grading. But that system was changed to the more traditional one of A's, B's, etc. Although I wasn't interested in putting too much emphasis on grades, I did want grades to accurately reflect the value of the students' work. I found that students were surprised, and dismayed, when their B work got only B's and only a few outstanding students received A's. Then the complaints began. "I've never received any grade lower than an A." "What do you expect from me, I did the best I could." "I'm only going to be an elementary school teacher, how well do I have to be able to write?" When I was about to give one mediocre student a C, the dean interceded. Anything less than a B– is considered a failing grade in the grad school. The dean pulled me aside and gave me the facts of life, pointing out that the student's father was a donor to the college and adding, "We don't want to ruin the self-esteem of our future teachers." I struggled against the culture for a while, but after a couple of years I couldn't stand the pressure and gave mostly A's like everyone else.
> —Former instructor, Wheelock College graduate school

Self-esteem seems to have replaced academic rigor even at the top schools, such as Harvard, where about half of all students get a grade of A– or above. (In the Harvard College Class of 2001, 90 percent of the students graduating received the mention Honors, High Honors or Highest Honors.)[4] As the *Economist* pointed out, "American students now take for granted that they will be given an A for the work that twenty years ago would have got a C." The writer lays the blame on two factors, one being "the cloying culture of self-esteem that stretches well beyond Harvard," and the other the marketplace. "American universities are big businesses which can charge students in excess of $20,000 a year for the privilege of attending them. Students naturally gravitate towards institutions that are going to give them a return on their investment—the sparkling academic resume which opens doors. . . . Professors who resist the demand for grade-inflation may find themselves embarrassed by empty classrooms. Study course guides provide plenty of details about how generously teachers grade."[5]

> Every semester students evaluated the courses we taught. They filled blue pages of evaluative type questions with their opinions on our every move, every activity, every foible. At the beginning of each semester, students would mill around the large three-ring evaluation notebooks that line the top shelf of a low bookcase in the Gutman Library, considering what courses to sign up for. Faculty members were always wary of what our students wrote about us. And we knew that students complained bitterly when we graded them too low. So I found myself being careful of the criticisms I made, and graded them less rigorously than I might have. It was a real conundrum—how to be true to myself and how to be fair to the students—and the bottom line, how to keep my job.
> —Former instructor, Harvard Graduate School of Education

One hundred sixty years after the founding of normal schools, there is nothing remotely resembling a national consensus on the question of how best to train teachers, even among teacher educators. Despite numerous and varied efforts to examine critically the sagging quality of teacher education and reform it, teacher preparation institutions remain remarkably resistant to substantive change. According to Seymour Sarason, Yale University professor emeritus and an authority on school culture and school reform, "It is truly remarkable how cosmetic the changes have been, amounting to little more than add-ons to conformity-reinforcing programs."[6] This is one of our less than inspiring stories:

Typically, it's part of a student teacher's preparation to spend a small amount of time in a "real" classroom under the tutelage of a veteran teacher. These budding educators are virtually parachuted into their training classroom by a college or university, in order to complete their education with a semester or so of "practice teaching," which happens toward the end of their last year in teacher education. Coordination and communication between college and public school are minimal, where they exist at all.

Our poster girl for inept student teachers was Lola Graham, a graduate student at Lesley College (real school, fictional names). It didn't take us long to discover that lovely Lola couldn't find Guatemala on a map of the world. She couldn't spell the word *excellent*. And, in spite of many hours of intensive coaching on our part, she couldn't control the class. She was incapable of connecting her college training to her real-life classroom. She wanted to teach poetry when we were doing a project on New World exploration. Why? Her college instructor had taught her how to prepare a lesson on poetry but hadn't taught her how to prepare a lesson on explorers (she complained), so she insisted we give her the chance to teach poetry. Vivian and I spent long hours with Lola after school, reviewing her lessons, suggesting strategies that would have worked better, pushing her to think more deeply about what she was teaching and how she was teaching it. Nothing worked. Trying to teach Lola how to be a classroom teacher was futile. Clearly, she belonged in another vocation.

So we approached Carleton Caruso, Lola's supervisor at Lesley. We laid out the problem and told Carleton that Lola, sweet child that she was, had no place in the classroom, and we couldn't, in good conscience, recommend her for classroom teaching. We wanted to flunk her out of the program. Carleton was livid. "You have to sign off on her, you *have* to!" he exploded.

"Don't you have any standards?" Vivian howled. He ranted. We raved. It was fruitless. I would like to say that we fought our case all the way up to the Supreme Court, but we didn't. We buckled. We were up against a tradition-bound culture in which teachers, unlike physicians, play no meaningful role in determining the quality of those who enter the profession. Our job was to provide the best training we could and then rubber-stamp the college administrators' resolve to put virtually any graduate who could breathe (we called it the mirror test) into some classroom somewhere. It was a defining moment when we realized that any attempt to improve the quality of classroom teachers had to acknowledge the flawed relationship between the universities and the public schools.

—Kitty

Unfortunately, a painful history accompanies past attempts at cooperation between universities and public schools. Few elementary and secondary teachers have escaped being demeaned by universities during their careers. And few university faculty members who have worked closely with schools have escaped being scratched up in the briar patch of public schools. Historically, schools have been inhospitable places for academics. It is as if both school and university people harbor antibodies they have built up to guard against being infected with each other's culture.

Efforts to change this relationship and create symbiotic partnerships between universities and schools are now being attempted. These partnerships, known as professional development schools (PDS's) and modeled on the philosophy of the teaching hospital, are alliances between a college or university and a K–12 school. PDS's are dedicated to student achievement, to the clinical preparation of new teachers, and to research directed at the improvement of teaching practice. They are designed to provide an intensive clinical environment in which teachers and university faculty share responsibility for student and teacher learning. The heart of the PDS idea is to improve the preparation and continuing education of educators. We believe that professional development schools are a good idea, although difficult in practice. Still, even where PDS programs are successfully run, and they are few, universities take no real responsibility for the teaching competency of their graduates.

It is common knowledge that institutions that train teachers tend to treat their education programs as "cash cows" and divert tuition dollars paid by education majors to law, medicine, business, engineering, and other programs. Those programs, in other words, which will provide a better return in building prestige for the university and in attracting dollars from wealthy alumni. Graduates of the education schools don't often sign large checks to build libraries and football stadiums.

> It's no secret that schools of education are at the bottom of the university pecking order. And that on the bottom rung of the education school's own ladder of prestige are those who actually train teachers.[7]

As Stanford University professor Linda Darling-Hammond notes: "If you are preparing to be a teacher, you can expect [only] about half of the tuition money you put into the till to come back to support your preparation."[8] As a result, students are placed in large classes rather than intensive, more expensive clinical internships. The part-time faculty is disproportionate, and full-time education faculty members—even those with big names and solid reputations in the field—receive far lower salaries than their counterparts in other departments. The end result is a shamefully high tolerance for mediocrity and substandard training in both academic content and pedagogy that ill-prepares young women and men for the realities of classroom life. The pattern of mediocrity and incompetence begins in schools of education with courses like Math for Teachers (read "math for dummies") and infects the entire system.

Most states don't even require schools of education to be accredited. As a result, only 500 out of 1,300 of those schools meet what we consider to be minimal professional standards.[9]

In many ways the education of today's teachers is almost as weak as it was for doctors in 1910. Physicians did not always meet the high standards to which they are held today. In the nineteenth century, medical practice in the United States was largely unregulated and any citizen could call himself a doctor. To promote the establishment of licensing laws, the Carnegie Foundation commissioned Abraham Flexner (not a doctor but an educator) to examine the nation's medical schools and make recommendations for their improvement. His damning report in 1910 sparked a revolution in American medical education.

Flexner concluded that physicians were poorly selected and trained in unscientific "diploma mills." As a result of Flexner's work, states ultimately closed all undergraduate schools of medicine and made the training of doctors a postgraduate course for the brightest college graduates.

In contrast, here's what a young woman has to say about her graduate program at Teachers College at Columbia University. After graduating from Harvard, she pursued her master's degree at Columbia at the same time her husband was in medical school there.

> The year I was at T.C., my husband was in his third year of medical school. He was doing rotations in the hospital . . . getting hands-on experience working with patients under real doctors. Medical students were expected to do a lot, putting in I.V.'s, doing physical exams; they threw him in but there was always a team, one or two steps ahead to point out what he was doing right or not. That never happened to me in teacher education. He studied pharmacology, learning something like 250 medications. Then he had to learn what he should use, when to use them, what the contraindications were. I remembered quizzing him on it. I asked him recently if he really needed all that stuff, and he said, "Absolutely." I envy his having a real knowledge base and I don't feel that I have that.
>
> One of our seminars, given once a week for three hours, was described to us as "the backbone of our teacher training experience." A lot of the three hours was spent writing with magic markers on easel pads, in order to "share our own experiences." Like, when were you humiliated? When were you proud? Whenever we did a practicing of what we were going to teach in the classroom, we practiced on each other. Adults, acting like children, pretending to learn, while other adults were pretending to teach. I thought it was ridiculous. And I paid $30,000 for it.

Another graduate of Columbia relates a similar complaint.

The methods courses were the worst. In the math methods course titled Mathematics in Elementary Schools, we would do workshops that were taught like an elementary math course. The whole course was a review of long division and fractions—and we were tested on that. We were taught using pattern blocks: not how to use them with kids, but how to use them ourselves, pretending we were fourth graders. To have to review and take a test on long division and fractions, that was a complete waste of time.

Here we have a picture of acute dysfunction, a system seemingly immune to internal or external reform—a market-driven machine that accommodates underqualified candidates, exploits them for their dollar value, and then pours undereducated and poorly trained teachers into your children's classrooms. Because no general agreement exists about what it is that teachers need to know, teacher education is a blank check written by consumers to those who suffer no accountability.

The growth and increasing diversity of the nation's student population, the avalanche of teacher retirements in the coming decade, the strength of the nation's economy and its dependence on a well-educated population, and the appalling shortage of national leadership in the training of teachers all point to an extraordinary reform opportunity available to teacher training institutions. It is an opportunity that has so far gone begging.

Certification Requirements Are Nearly Irrelevant

Even where the universities, colleges, and numerous other teacher preparation programs fall down on the job, you might expect that the teacher certification regulations, legally mandated in every state, would act as a filter to prevent poorly prepared or unqualified teachers from entering the classrooms of America. You would be wrong. The laws of supply and demand exert enormous pressures to put teachers into classrooms, regardless of their qualifications. Although regulations for teacher certification exist in every state, they are less stringent, for example, than those for lifeguards, accountants, hairdressers, cosmeticians, opticians, plumbers, and other people who are licensed to deliver services to the general public.

On top of that, existing regulations are inconsistently enforced, and often waived or abandoned entirely, under the pressure to recruit bodies to put in front of children. There *must* be a teacher in every classroom. When certified teachers are unavailable, regulations go out the window. More than forty states allow school districts to hire teachers on emergency licenses who have not met the basic state requirements. In desperate schools all over the country (and this is not an extreme example) art teachers and high school football coaches are assigned to teach science and math classes. When the supply of teacher candidates that fulfill even minimal requirements dries up, then requirements are lowered further, ignored, or worked around. Numerous strategies are employed.

Recently, the Arkansas Board of Education gave state education officials the flexibility to waive tests of general skills and content knowledge for nontraditional candidates and also to waive the 2.75 GPA requirement (a C+ in one of the least demanding curriculums imaginable) for teacher candidates coming out of college.[10] In other words, if you have a college degree and can demonstrate modest proficiency in some area, you can pretty much be assured of a job teaching in Arkansas.

Georgia's new Teach for Georgia program has opened that state's classrooms to college graduates who have a 2.5 GPA, can pass a basic skills test, and take a four-week "orientation" course.[11]

Alaska is working to pass legislation that would allow anyone to get a job as a public school teacher who has a bachelor's degree in a subject area or has been employed in that field for five years or has two years' substitute teaching experience.[12]

For a standard license, some states require a degree in the subject to be taught, courses in education, practice teaching, and continuing course work leading to a master's degree. Other states require less than a minor in a subject area, a few weeks of student teaching, and a couple of education courses.

All over the country, state boards of education are struggling with strategies to recruit teachers by lowering the requirements for hiring (as well as providing cash incentives and other lures such as cruises and paid vacation trips). At the same time, in a paradox that seems to have eluded any serious discussion, state legislators are proposing to raise teacher and student performance with tough teacher testing and high-stakes testing of students. In other words, hire less-qualified people and then hold them to higher standards, while making their jobs nearly impossible.

The appeal of modest policy changes is that they cost very little, are easy to implement, and do not require expensive research and development. They merely serve as public relations mechanisms. See! The legislators of your state are *doing something!* Unfortunately these misguided, short-term solutions often carry great potential for further undermining the quality of classroom teaching. In the end, we all know who suffers the most.

Without telling parents, many districts hire unqualified people as teachers and assign them full responsibility for children. More than 12 percent of all newly hired "teachers" arrive in the classroom without any appropriate training at all, and another 15 percent enter without having fully met state standards.[13] Some statistics:

- More than 50,000 people who lack the training for their jobs enter teaching *every year* on emergency or substandard licenses.[14]
- As many as 30 percent of all classroom teachers in the United States do not meet the minimal standards required by the regulations in their states.[15]
- Nearly 25 percent of all secondary school teachers (30 percent for math) do not have even a college minor in their main teaching field.[16]

- Among teachers who teach a second subject, 36 percent are unlicensed in the field and 50 percent lack a minor.[17]
- In schools with high minority enrollments, students have less than a 50 percent chance of getting a science or math teacher who holds a degree and a license in the field in which she or he teaches.[18]
- Only 30 percent of teachers feel well prepared to use technology in their classrooms.[19]

Attempting to find new sources for teacher recruitment (thereby speeding up the process of putting unqualified people into classrooms), some policy makers advocate the abolition of formal teacher preparation altogether; some argue for simple apprenticeships, short courses of instruction as alternative routes to teacher certification. Many state departments of education react to the teacher shortage by advocating the elimination of education degrees and certification requirements that they claim prevent knowledgeable and educated people from entering the profession. It never seems to occur to people who propose these ideas that teaching is a difficult skill that requires intensive training, practice, and professional development. Would someone who proposes to put an uncertified teacher in a classroom ever think of having his gall bladder removed by an amateur who happened to achieve success in some other field? We doubt it. Yet, these folks are enthusiastic about having unskilled teachers perform education "operations" on your children.

Numerous schemes have been proposed for providing alternative pathways for prospective teachers to fill empty teaching slots. Alternative programs ranging from Teach for America to revised certification programs organized by states and local school districts have become increasingly widespread and continue to attract growing numbers of teaching candidates.

Teach for America, begun in 1989 by a Princeton student, is one of the largest single producers of new teachers. Recruits from more than 160 colleges and universities enroll in a six-week preservice summer institute. Practice teaching at local schools is followed by a two-week supervised induction at a selected school site. Thereafter, graduates are placed as full-fledged teachers at urban and rural schools, with a minumum two-year guarantee of employment. They are paid the same salary as any beginning teacher, plus a $9,500 bonus if they complete the full two years. About 17 percent drop out before completing their two-year tour. Of those who fulfill their commitment, only 22 percent elect to stay in the field of education—and few of those in the classroom.[20]

The concept reminds us of the accelerated OCS (officer candidate school) program of World War II, which was created in response to the shortage of first lieutenants. Officers were being killed off faster than they could be trained. So the army simply speeded up the course of training in order to produce lieutenant-grade officers in only three months. Graduates were scornfully called ninety-day wonders. Some were successful in leading their men into battle, but many were not. Some rose to the challenge and became fine officers. Some were killed right off the boat. Some got their men killed rather quickly, as well. Some, it is rumored, were such disasters as leaders that they were shot in the back by their own men.

To be fair, Teach for America (TFA) enjoys a certain measure of success, and the negative results are not quite so drastic as those in the OCS—most TFA teachers emerge from the program intact. A few do remain in teaching, but not many. It is a noble effort by well-intentioned young people who view their stint as public service, sweetened with the opportunity to earn a bonus that helps pay off their student loans. There is no research to indicate whether these recruits' effect on students has been any different from that of similarly undertrained novices from other backgrounds who come into the classroom. Teach for America supplies a constant stream of novice teachers who look on their tenure as helping an urban or rural school on a short-term basis. These are teaching temps who do little to improve the quality of classroom instruction. An article in *Educa-*

tional Leadership points out that "the sense of frustration in not knowing how to meet students' needs drives many potentially good teachers out of teaching."[21] A Yale University graduate who had entered the Teach for America program with high ideals says of his experience:

> I, perhaps like most TFA-ers, harbored dreams of liberating my students from public school mediocrity and offering them as good an education as I had received. But I was not ready. . . . I was not a successful teacher, and the loss to the students was real and large.[22]

The teacher shortage has proven to be an economic boon for teacher recruitment agencies. Visiting International Faculty, a for-profit clearinghouse based in Chapel Hill, North Carolina, began as a cultural exchange program but now actively recruits teachers from foreign countries for placement in U.S. classrooms—at a fee of $11,500 for each teacher hired. In the school year 2000–01, VIF recruited 1,300 teachers from thirty-five countries for schools in eight states. In the 2001–02 school year, it expects to place 1,800 to 2,000 teachers.[23]

The New York City Board of Education has hired math and science teachers from Austria; Chicago's school system brought in seventy-one teachers from twenty-eight countries, including Hungary and China, this past year; and Houston officials welcomed eleven new teachers from Russia. School officials in Fulton County, Georgia, actively recruited in Australia, New Zealand, South Africa, and Jamaica. It is expected that Florida's Palm Beach County will see an influx of teachers recruited from the Philippines.[24]

Aside from questions regarding the certification of foreign teachers, which are troubling to education officials and teachers' unions alike, there is the concern that recruiting teachers from other countries reduces the pressure on government bodies to address the teacher shortage through increases in training, pay, and other benefits for teachers already in place.[25]

In belated response to the acknowledged deterioration in the quality of teacher candidates, some states have begun to require some form of testing for a teacher's license. When teacher testing came to Massachusetts in 1998, 59 percent of all teacher candidates failed the first round.[26] Unsurprisingly, teacher testing is routinely resisted by the unions.

Other initiatives in teacher education abound. The most noteworthy recommend higher academic standards, closer university ties with schools and school districts, varied experiences for preservice teachers in schools over the course of their academic career, and active involvement by teachers and school administrators in the education of the next generation of schoolteachers. Doane College in Crete, Nebraska, goes so far as to offer a guarantee to the employing school system. If the school finds that the new teacher is deficient, the college will allow the person to take additional courses to improve his or her skills without charge. This approach is commendable, and rare.

Most "Professional Development" Is Weak and Ineffective

A teacher friend of ours had her kitchen completely remodeled and when it was finished invited us over for a cup of coffee so we could admire the results. "You might be interested in this," she said, as we sat on stools at her gleaming new granite counter, "About a month ago I stepped into this mess of hammering and whirling sawdust to overhear a conversation between the contractor and his head carpenter. They were talking about a workshop they were going to in Connecticut given by a big manufacturer of expensive kitchen cabinets. The workshop was about installation tips and techniques as well as ways to apply those techniques to the manufacturer's product line. Wow, I thought. Here are two guys who probably have a lot of other things they could be doing on a weekend but are attending what amounts to a course in *professional development*."

Our friend also related how the carpenters talked about what they thought they were going to get out of the course, how they could apply it to their jobs, and how they could pass on the information they learned to the other carpenters they were working with when they were installing this manufacturer's cabinets on the next job they had—which was already scheduled. Although they would not have used that term, professional development was in their view an ongoing process in which they acquired information that would help them do their jobs better, leading (we assume) to a higher degree of professionalism, better status, and increased income. Clearly, they thought it was something they needed to do and that it would bring them benefits.

In the world of education, professional development—also called staff development or in-service training—is the continuing education of teachers. Some have broadened the definition to incorporate the sum total of learning experiences throughout a teacher's career. In that sense, as one educator has put it, professional development goes beyond the term *training,* with its implication of learning skills, and encompasses a definition that includes formal and informal means of helping teachers not only learn new skills but also develop new insights into pedagogy and their own practice, and explore new or advanced understandings of content and resources.[27]

In other words, it is assumed that teachers need to upgrade their skills, learn new methods, keep current about emerging trends in education, acquire information on how to implement changes in curriculum, and in general continually improve their teaching.

Although school districts typically expend only 2 to 3 percent of their annual budgets on staff development (minuscule by business standards), professional development still represents hundreds of millions of dollars spent on untold workshops, programs, college courses, and seminars. Professional development is a huge topic in public education, much discussed. Standards for professional development, both narrow and broad, abound. The New Jersey Professional Teaching Standards Board, for example, lists fifty-eight standards for "professional development plans [to be] created by the local professional development committees in school districts. These standards . . . provide guidance for the successful completion of the professional development requirements."[28] Professional development is built into education legislation, union contracts, college curricula, and state mandates. Many an education consultant's career is nourished (as, at times, ours have been) by travel across the continent or around the globe to deliver "professional development" services. Make no mistake about it: in terms of the time and money spent on it and attention paid to it, professional development is a very big deal.

Mostly, though, it's a sham. Patricia Graham, former dean of the Harvard Graduate School of Education gets it just about right, we think, when she says "Professional development for teachers, as we currently define it, is foolishness."[29] In our view, foolishness is too mild a word.

> There is no research evidence that professional development makes a difference. . . . The studies are not very good that professional development works.
> —Professor, Harvard Graduate School of Education

> Currently, local districts spend a great deal on professional development—and it is typically spent in ineffective ways for unclear reasons. . . . There is no consensus in the field about best practice in professional development. . . . There is a growing body of opinion among "experts" that the conventional forms of professional development are virtually a waste of time. . . . information delivery and training are too isolated from classroom realities to have an impact on teachers' practice.[30]

Keep the phrase "too isolated from classroom realities to have an impact" firmly in mind. This is at the very heart of why professional development, as it is currently delivered, has had so little effect and why teachers themselves are so often cynical about its practice. Here is what a few classroom teachers have told us:

I can get an increase in salary just by taking courses on almost anything. Credits add up, and when they reach a certain point, I get a pay increase. The course doesn't have to have a direct connection to my subject matter or direct application to teaching. I can take a course at my local college in gardening or stress management and it counts as professional development credits, or even toward a master's degree.

There's a wide variety of choices, and little quality control. More and more states ask that teachers be recertified, but loose guidelines mean that just about any course can be used to fulfill recertification requirements.

Professional development is pretty much a waste of time, but we have to do it. It's a one size fits all approach . . . the same professional development session for all third grade teachers, even though some have taught two or three years and others in the room are twenty-year veterans.

Outside experts who haven't taught in a million years are hired to give inservice training. The experts are supposed to do the thinking while teachers are reduced to doing the implementing. Professional development is often a "deficit model." It assumes that teachers are in need of "fixing" and it doesn't recognize the value of the teacher's knowledge of curriculum and pedagogy.

In most cases, professional development is thought of as formal education activities or workshops, similar in nature to those mentioned by our friend's carpenters. When professional development is appropriate to the specific experience and work life of a particular teacher, it can be effective and rewarding, within certain limitations. Most often, however, it is not even remotely related to a teacher's professional development needs. Seldom is there any follow-up or continuity, and information delivered today may contradict that given previously. In our experience, teachers' disillusionment with professional development is nearly universal:

I can recall the countless professional development workshops and seminars I've attended during my five years of teaching. During those seminars, that typically took place outside of school, I sat with hundreds of teachers as we listened carefully to someone tell us "how to teach." After each seminar I returned to my classroom only to add that seminar's instruction packet to my already full and dusty bookshelf. Lack of time, confidence, and experience prevented me from trying to put the strategies and ideas I had heard about in my seminar into practice.

Professional development is so faddish—the flavor of the month club. This year's interest in math means that all our in-service is around the conceptual understanding of numbers—never, no never, teach the kids a math fact. But we know that in a couple of years it's back to teaching math facts in kindergarten. In reading it was the same—five years ago it was "whole language," as if phonics would damage the child. Now the pendulum has swung back to phonics. The philosophies that we're made to listen to change with the weather. And each new curriculum is almost sure to be the opposite of what we were told to do before or are teaching now. And we're all handed it as if we're novices who haven't taught for very long.

The failures of professional development aren't due to any lack of diligent attention to the problem. Lots of smart people, understanding the huge waste of time and money being poured into ineffective programs, have thoroughly investigated the whole spectrum of professional development conundrums and arrived at intelligent, well-reasoned solutions. The Center for Policy Research in Education, for example, contends[31] that professional development would be effective *if* it took place

- Where teachers worked together, sharing ideas and responsibilities and enjoying exchanges of information that included joint discussions of their practice
- Where teacher networks provided access to a "professional community" in which their expertise and experience were respected and where they could be active participants in a professional discourse about improving their practice

- Where schools and colleges collaborated effectively to create and implement teacher training and professional development programs
- Where professional development schools, based on the model of the teaching hospital, brought novice and experienced teachers together with college faculty to improve professional practice through observation, experimentation, reflection, and coaching
- Where teachers themselves, in cooperation with colleagues and college faculty, are engaged in education research that informs their practice
- Where teachers meet the standards of certification proposed by the National Board for Professional Teaching Standards (NBPTS),[32] a process which in itself would provide a considerable amount of professional development.

Altogether, that's a mighty big if. Too big in today's world, in fact, given that those conditions never all pertain in one place at one time. Teachers most often work in an environment of isolation rather than collaboration. Successful school-college collaborations are rare. Teachers are not usually networked into a professional community. Teachers are only just beginning to learn the practice and value of teacher research, and it is not universally encouraged or supported. NBPTS certification, while widely respected, is difficult to attain, and so far fewer than 1 percent of all classroom teachers hold that certification.

Professional development *could* play a vital role in providing teachers—especially those who have been identified as being undertrained—with the support and learning opportunities that could make a very real difference in their effectiveness as teachers. It is most unfortunate that at the very time in the history of teaching when a robust infrastructure of professional development programs is most needed and could do the most good, it just isn't there.

Not enough
academically able
students are being
drawn to teaching

The professional
life of teachers is
on the whole
unacceptable

Teacher prepara-
tion programs
need substantial
improvement

Poor Working Conditions Drive Teachers out of the Classroom

4 Mamas, Don't Let Your Babies Grow Up to Be Teachers

I don't see any reason why a garbage collector shouldn't be paid more than a teacher. It's a very unattractive job, whereas teaching is very attractive.—John Silber, as chairman of the Massachusetts Board of Education

---

There's a mournfully humorous country-western tune that warns mothers against letting their babies grow up to be cowboys.[1] The song implores them to encourage their children to become doctors or lawyers instead. Yes, let them be doctors or lawyers, but not teachers. We're not likely, at least not any time soon, to hear a song encouraging mothers to guide their children into teaching. Teaching is a job fraught with frustration—a dead-end vocation with no career path, low pay, low status, and poor working conditions.

> I was talking to a group of Arts and Sciences faculty members at a forum to discuss the crisis in teacher recruitment. I asked them to raise their hands if they were telling their best students to consider a career in teaching. Not a single hand went up. I know they're looking at their best students and telling them to go to grad school. We can be pretty sure

that they're telling their lowest students, "If you can't do anything else, you can always teach."

—Researcher, Education Trust

Take This Job

How many people would willingly study for and enter a career if they knew beforehand that their first day on the job would be very much like their last, thirty or forty years later? Can such a job even be called a career? The only way for a teacher to move up is to move out—and into a job as principal, superintendent, or central office administrator. Some "graduate" to teaching in higher education or leave education entirely.

> I had been teaching for three years when my second child was born, and I was looking for a job share. . . . a principal who knew I was looking called to offer me a job as a reading specialist. It wasn't what I was looking for. . . . I loved classroom teaching . . . but I just wanted to lighten my work load until my children got a little older. I talked to my mother about my conflict and she said, go ahead and take it, it'll be a step up and open new opportunities for you. As a teacher I had always thought that reading specialists didn't work as hard because they didn't have an entire class to manage, just to focus on a single child . . . but the outside world thinks when a teacher leaves the classroom it's a promotion. It's "stepping up."
>
> —Reading specialist, former teacher

Teaching offers no promotions, and pay raises are based almost exclusively on years of service or earned academic degrees (which in most states can be in an unrelated or irrelevant subject area). There are therefore no external incentives or rewards for acquiring knowledge, sharpening skills, or improving performance.

It is no secret that teachers are poorly paid. In the United States, teachers earn less, in terms of income in relation to gross national product, than their counterparts in many other industrialized nations, yet they spend far more hours in front of the classroom. Internationally, for example, the average salary of a teacher with fifteen years' experience (as a percentage of average per capita income) is 136 percent. It is 250 percent in South Korea, 160 percent in Greece, 128 percent in France, but 99 percent in the United States. Moreover, because American teachers have a heavier workload, their hourly pay averages only $35, as compared with the earnings of a South Korean teacher—$77 an hour. The same *New York Times* article, reporting on the study, notes that "salary differentials are part of a pattern of relatively low public investment in education in the United States compared with other . . . nations." Teacher salaries account for 56 percent of what the United States pays for education, well below the 67 percent average among the thirty member nations of the Organization for Economic Cooperation and Development (OECD).[2]

"The good news is that salaries of teachers are improving," claims the National Education Association.[3] Well, we don't know what they mean by "improving," except to note that while salaries may be increasing, the dollar value of teachers' salaries in real income has continued to decline over the past decade.

In relative terms, increases in pay for teachers have lagged far behind those in other professions, and the pay scales in general are pitiful. Beginning teachers are paid far less than college graduates of engineering, chemistry, math, accounting, business administration, sales and marketing, and liberal arts. In 1997 the average beginning salary for a teacher with a bachelor's degree and no experience was $25,000, and the average pay was $38,436. A beginning teacher can look forward to doubling her salary in thirty years. At the same time, it is not unusual for graduates of, say, a business school, to double their salary in just a few years, perhaps quadrupling it in ten. Should that business school graduate rise to the level of a CEO, he or she could expect to make 458 times that of the average worker.[4]

To add insult to injury, a third of the teachers in the United States will not qualify for Social Security benefits at retirement, because their states have chosen not to have their teachers join the Social Security system. Why? It saves the states money. In some cases, teachers may receive Social Security benefits if they have also worked at jobs other than teaching, for 58 percent of public school teachers rely on supplemental income gained by working weekends, summers, and outside school hours. This means that the job's most attractive perk—summer vacations—is unavailable to many teachers trapped by economic necessity.

It must be said, however, that although poor salaries may keep otherwise interested candidates from entering teaching, those who leave because of low pay are in the minority. To cite an example, in a study conducted by education officials in Michigan among teachers who had recently quit, fewer than 9 percent cited salary concerns. Two-thirds laid the blame on lack of administrative support and inattention to their needs. Asked why he thought so many teachers were leaving the public schools in Arkansas, which faces a crisis in teacher retention, a member of the state board of education said that "many teachers feel they lack the support they need from the school, students, parents, and communities."[5]

As the Rodney Dangerfields of the professional class, teachers get no respect and little acknowledgment of their accomplishments. Josh Shulman, an excellent fourth grade teacher in Brookline, Massachusetts, was teaching his class about the American Revolution, the first Native Americans who provided the settlers with corn, the foundations of colonial government, and the origins of the Commonwealth of Massachusetts . . . how a government is formed and how laws are enacted. To demonstrate the process of initiative petition, the procedure by which a citizen's initiative can get passed into law, the class decided to make the corn muffin the "official muffin" of Massachusetts. The project was an enormous success and, indeed, their initiative petition got passed into law. The media got wind of the story, and it appeared in local television and newspaper reports. Then it hit the "Today Show," and kids were interviewed on national television.

Not once was Josh interviewed; not once was his name mentioned; not once did anyone say, Gosh, wasn't that a great thing for a teacher to do. It was as if, somehow, a brilliant class of fourth graders had thought the project up all by themselves, written the petition, and gotten the law passed all on their own, and the teacher had no role in the enterprise whatsoever. Over the years, we've noticed this phenomenon over and over again. Kids appear on television for something wonderful their class has done. Never is the teacher mentioned. Why are teachers invisible?

The notion that if someone teaches in a public school rather than in a college, that person must be of a lower intelligence is pervasive and, unless you are subjected to the subtle humiliation that this sort of prejudice inevitably produces, even faintly comic. If you teach in a university, you are thought to be brilliant. If you teach first grade, people marvel at your ability to tie your own shoes and speak in complete sentences. Respect for teachers is a spectrum, from the highest level, the Mt. Olympus of university professors, to the lowly ranks of elementary school teachers. The attitude affects conversational tone, as well as assumptions of competency.

> When Kitty and I both taught graduate courses—she at Harvard and I at Wheelock—we would play this game at conferences. As we introduced ourselves we would first say we were fourth grade teachers . . . and then allow a small pause before continuing ". . . and we also teach at [Wheelock, Harvard]." It was interesting to observe the difference in reaction—and we saw this dozens of times—when to the question "What do you do?" we responded with "teach fourth grade" or "teach in the Graduate School of Education at Harvard University." You could actually see a person's body language and facial expression change in mid-sentence.
> —Vivian

Teachers suffer the worst working conditions of any so-called professional. Here we are, at the dawn of a new millennium, and most teachers have no telephones, no fax machines, no personal com-

puters, and limited access to copiers. Teachers line up at the one or
two phones available to them to make calls to parents during the
school day. In many schools, the shortage of textbooks and materials
is critical.

Teaching has become increasingly dangerous, unhealthy, and un-
pleasant. In the 1993–94 school year, 5 percent of all *elementary*
school teachers reported having been physically attacked by a student. Over the five-year period from 1992 through 1996, teachers
were the victims of 1,581,000 nonfatal crimes at school, including
962,000 thefts and 619,000 violent crimes (rape or sexual assault,
robbery, aggravated assault, and simple assault).[6]

The buildings in which teachers work are not always maintained
in good condition. The National Education Association estimates
that 60 percent of all schools in America are in need of major repairs.[7]
School systems often elect to postpone repairs and delay construction
of new facilities to save money, not only during periods of financial
austerity, but in times of prosperity as well, in order to keep tax rates
down. When money is tight, maintenance costs are often slashed
first. In prosperous times, when the public coffers are full, politicians
give tax breaks to win political favor instead of putting money into
the educational infrastructure. Deferring maintenance results in
building deterioration, indoor air problems, increased repair costs,
and reduced operating efficiency of equipment. Making cuts in up-
keep and replacement costs is considered less devastating than slash-
ing academic programs, but the result of such decisions is that the
overall condition of school facilities in the United States is deteriorat-
ing. In many American schools, students and teachers find themselves in a physical environment that adversely affects their morale
and, in some cases, their health. A 1992 national survey conducted by
the American Association of School Administrators found that 74
percent of school facilities should be replaced or repaired immediately; an additional 12 percent were identified as inadequate places
for learning. In a similar study, one in four schools reported that at

least one type of on-site building was in less than adequate condition. Fifty percent of the schools reported that at least one of the building's features (plumbing, heating, ventilation, and so on) was in less than adequate condition. Seventy-five percent reported needing to spend money to restore their school building to "good overall condition." The total amount needed by schools was estimated to be approximately $127 billion. Nonetheless, in its most recent session Congress declined to pass legislation to modernize schools.[8]

Less and less of a teacher's time is spent actually teaching children. A significant part of a teacher's work week is spent on nonteaching activities, such as menial housekeeping or clerical duties. Almost all elementary school teachers are responsible for monitoring the playground or cafeteria, activities that are nothing more than babysitting. In the school where we formerly worked, in a well-to-do suburb of Boston, teachers are assigned to spray tables in the cafeteria. Almost all teachers have to stand in line at the copy machine (when it is working), make their own teaching tools, and often purchase their own materials. The average teacher spends $408 per year of her or his own money on texts, materials, and classroom supplies. Teachers have to come in on days early in the fall—on their own time—to organize, clean, and set up their classrooms, and stay at the end of the school year to put their books and supplies away, stack chairs, and rearrange the furniture they arranged at the beginning of the year, again on their own time. Teachers work an average of forty-nine hours per week, and eleven of those hours are uncompensated.[9]

For the beginning teacher, life is especially difficult. In contrast to the office worker, who is likely to be escorted to a clean desk on the first day and given the requisite supplies, the beginning teacher is in for a shock. She will probably enter a room where scavengers have made off with everything of value and left her with torn books, broken chairs, and a miscellaneous assortment of discarded desks and furniture. As the new kid on the block, she will not have had time to curry favor with the custodian and the guardian of the supply closet, so it will be a while before she has nearly the materials and equipment she needs. She has entered a culture in which it takes years to build one's own cache of supplies, to be guarded jealously. In reality, this is not much different from the experience of novices in other professions who are forced to deal with rites of initiation—new lawyers, for example, who get stuck with boring cases and medical interns who must empty bedpans. Aside from the annoyance of housekeeping, a beginning teacher faces a far more serious obstacle to success, and one that makes no sense. She will be given the most challenging kids in her grade level—the troublemakers, the low achievers, the kids with special needs—all the castoffs the other teachers don't want to deal with. The problem kids who demand the greatest skill and experience to handle get the teacher with the most to learn and the least to fall back on (in the way of acumen). The teacher who should encounter the easiest year of her career, one that would enable her to find a solid footing while gaining experience, is left in a minefield. The most experienced surgeons vie for the toughest challenges, the most experienced attorneys fight for the big cases, and the most experienced teachers use whatever leverage they possess to get the least troublesome kids.

Lacking support, any teacher—novice or veteran—is exceptionally vulnerable on different fronts. It's just that experienced teachers are slightly less likely to get into trouble. They know where the minefields are and can avoid them, with luck.

In Sharon, Massachusetts, a young, intelligent, and highly motivated teacher who was widely liked by parents and faculty gave a failing grade on a final exam to a student who had not bothered to take the test.

> I was a relatively new teacher in the system, and eager to do a good job. I thought that doing a good job meant teaching the best I could, and keeping standards high. . . . One year I gave an exam and one of my students just didn't show up. I gave her a failing grade on the exam. She came to me later and asked to make up the exam. I refused, and her

parents called me and asked me to give a makeup exam. I refused them, and they went to the principal and demanded that their daughter be allowed to take the makeup. The principal ordered me to drop the failing grade and replace it with the grade of the makeup. I was disgusted with the whole process, felt totally unsupported and disillusioned.

In New York City, a white first-year teacher was vilified as a racist by a group of black parents for using an award-winning children's book (by a black author) that included a word they felt was racist. They threatened the teacher and agitated for her removal, which was prompt. When the author of the book came publicly to the teacher's defense, and an inquiry showed that the charge of racism was baseless, she was invited to come back to her class; by then she was teaching in another school, and her faith in her former principal and the administration was shattered. No one in authority defended this teacher when she was attacked. The knee-jerk reaction was to jettison the teacher rather than face up to unreasonable parents. This is a typical response, and teachers suffer.[10]

Teaching Is an Isolated, Dead-End Job with No Career Path

Walk into just about any public elementary school during the day and you will see lots of people, both children and adults, engaged in conversations, interactions, and other forms of social discourse. Schools are busy places, so it may come as a surprise to learn that classroom teaching is a particularly lonely job. Teachers are cogs in a system that has institutionalized isolation and made it a normal condition of the work they do.

The problems of isolation lie at the root of the school culture that so powerfully shapes a teacher's work life, thwarts education reform, and ultimately degrades teaching.

The history of teaching has legitimized isolation, for today's schools are based on a model that is well over a hundred years old. The practice has been accepted for generations. If it is the "normal" condition of teaching, who would think of changing it? Certainly not teachers, who in study after study reveal that they have never considered teaching any way other than alone. The mental picture we all have of a teacher is of a solo practitioner, engaged in her craft inside a closed space, "her children" arranged before her, receiving her delivered wisdom. This image is so pervasive that it has become imprinted, like a genetic code, on the thoughts and habits of educators around the world—so much so that almost all attempts at education reform fail to take fully into account this central component of the teaching-learning process: the isolation of the classroom teacher.

Isolation is, in part, abetted by architecture.

For a brief period of my life I lived in a small town in Vermont. In many ways, rural Vermont recalls, at least visually, what life was like in eighteenth-century America. By today's standards Vermont is sparsely populated, but it was not always considered so. In 1976 there were about as many people living in Vermont as there were in 1776, except that in the eighteenth century that was considered a lot of people. They weren't concentrated in cities, however, but were spread out all over the state, on farms and in villages. This wide dispersal meant establishing a substantial number of one-room schoolhouses, some of which were still operating well into the twentieth century.

On a country walk with Chester, my seventy-six-year old neighbor who had lived all his life in the same town, we came upon a square, shallow depression in the ground, outlined with mossy stones and dappled with sunlight filtering through the trees. This was where a one-room schoolhouse had once stood. Chester said it was where he had gone to school as a child. It was late October, and a cold wind rustled the brittle leaves. I sat down on a large rock and listened, and felt alone. Isolated. What loneliness and isolation must have been the lot of the teacher in a one-room schoolhouse, I thought: no adults to talk to, no peers to consult, nowhere to go when you needed help. Just like teachers in classrooms today. For what are our classrooms now? Walled-off, one-room schoolhouses containing one grade and a single age group, stuck together in one building (the egg-crate structure), with the teachers inside still suffering from loneliness and isolation. This, along with the ramifications of the culture it breeds, is the major malady of "modern" public education.

—Kitty

Teachers continue to work alone in cell-like classrooms, separated from other teachers, in physical structures that resemble prisons and mental hospitals. Even in cases where school reform was attempted—when walls were torn down to encourage collaboration, teachers were so used to being separated that they moved file cabinets and book-cases to form walls between themselves and the teachers next to them. The prospect of losing their privacy and autonomy was too threatening. That wasn't the way they had been taught to teach, and most were given little advance notice of the "new way" of teaching. In the few instances where they were given some meager preparation, teachers eventually reverted to old habits anyway because the culture of the school had not changed in accommodation to the change in the physical environment. To a large degree, the physical environment of schools is a reflection of school culture, not the root cause of it.

The teacher's daily routine reinforces the isolation, because there is simply no time set aside in the schedule to interact with other teachers. When a teacher is not immediately involved in teaching children (inside four walls, with the door closed), she is planning and preparing—usually outside the school, and almost always alone. This is in sharp contrast to professions such as medicine or law, which are highly collaborative enterprises and demand intensive interaction and consultation among peers and up and down the hierarchy of rank. Consultation is built into the schedule of most physicians and attorneys, for whom it would be unthinkable, not to mention highly unprofessional, to gather information, make critical decisions, or carry out their practice entirely on their own.

Work overload, too, sustains isolation: teachers simply have too much to do. The undefined workload is implicit in the job of teaching. When higher-ups mandate that something new must be taught, rarely do they indicate what must be cut out of the school day to compensate for the addition. Teaching is an open-ended activity, and every classroom teacher is living proof of the truism that work expands to fill the time available. Every teacher knows that lesson plans can always be improved, students can always be given more individual attention, and homework can always be reviewed with greater care. Dealing directly with children is always more compelling than whatever else may compete for a teacher's time, and a teacher "knows" that no time is available to work with other teachers. In this way, isolation becomes a strategy for adapting to the demands of classroom teaching, and teachers actively strive to maintain and defend their time to themselves. Isolation, though, eliminates opportunities for teachers to expand their knowledge of their subject matter. Isolation undermines instructional quality by preventing the acquisition of knowledge and skills from other teachers with more experience and know-how. The net effect is that through her career, each teacher learns almost everything she knows by trial and error, from scratch. Teachers engage in what has been called parallel piecework, rarely if ever consulting with other teachers about their practice, plans, or methods. Teachers have few opportunities and little encouragement to work together and learn from one another.

My first teaching job was in a rural town in Arizona. Luckily, I found Ms. Ribicoff, a quiet woman who had great ideas for curriculum, and she helped me a lot. I went to her for advice on a regular basis, but her door was never open. She hid quietly in her room, afraid to become involved in even the smallest school issue. . . . it seemed to me that no one realized her talents and that I was the only one who looked to her as a mentor. I summoned up my courage to ask her why she was so reluctant to share her expertise. "I learned early on that you shut the door and don't cause trouble if you want to survive in schools" is what she said.
—Participant in a research study on teaching

When a teacher has a problem, she solves it by herself, or the problem remains unsolved. In most schools there is a strong taboo against entering another teacher's classroom, and this barrier is more than physical. Teachers neither offer nor seek another teacher's advice or counsel. Early in their careers, teachers are socialized to be intensely individualistic and private.

Teachers learn early that one does not ask for help. When they are hired, it is with the assumption that they know all they need to know. Should a teacher ask for help, a red flag is likely to go up among her colleagues. "She's in trouble," the signal is flashed, not "How can I help?" Seeking advice from other teachers is often considered an admission of incompetence.

The high standards of medicine and law bring with them the expectation that physicians and attorneys will attend conferences and seminars, constantly acquire new knowledge and skills, reflect on their practice, and enter into dialogue with other professionals. In the field of education, a good deal is said about professional development, but nearly all professional development programs for teachers are pathetically inadequate. If a teacher participates in a workshop or seminar that stresses the value of collaboration, he is ultimately stymied: school culture defeats any attempt to put those techniques into practice. Collaboration and teamwork are not the cultural norm.

A teacher can't think seriously about professional development or take steps to improve her practice unless she does so alone. Whereas professional development as an *idea* is widely encouraged, any teacher who attempts to put into practice what she has learned will find little support.

> The way to succeed in teaching is to be humble and subservient. I was never able to get things done. I wrote a grant together with the music teacher, Mr. Muraldo, so I could have a dance teacher in my classroom once a week. We got the grant, but because of scheduling conflicts it looked as if I couldn't participate. I spent more than a day running around consulting with teachers, flipping schedules. When I

got the logistical nightmare solved and ran it by the principal, she indignantly told me that scheduling was her job and I had no right to talk to teachers about schedules. I went to Mr. Muraldo, who explained that he would go to the principal and "stroke her." He said he had learned from the fourteenth century nun, Juana Inés de la Cruz, who was able to write letters to the bishop and have her ideas respected because she wrote from a base position. He [Muraldo] told me he always spoke to the principal as if he were her loyal and obedient servant.

—Elementary teacher, South Bronx

In the rigid school culture, star performance is discouraged by egalitarianism—the belief system that supports the preposterous premise that each teacher is the "equal" of any other teacher. Should any teacher try too hard or attract too much attention outside her classroom, she is likely to be subjected to the silently expressed put-down "Who does she think *she* is?" No cultural value is more stringently enforced than the status quo.

Egalitarianism is reinforced by a system that rewards (however poorly) only seniority financially, and not merit or knowledge or expertise or contributions to the profession, thereby lowering even further the status of teaching as an activity deserving of respect. If all teachers are equal, then none is outstanding, and there are no failures. The downside of egalitarianism is manifest from an interview we had with Suzanne, a graduate intern working in a Boston elementary school:

I spend time in a number of classrooms and am the most impressed with the strong teaching routine in Mrs. Santine's first grade class. The children are well behaved, always paying attention, . . . doing their work, always on task and never disruptive. One day I overheard the principal tell Mrs. Santine that it was clear her children were easier than those in the other first grade . . . that the administration needed to shift the "burden of behavior" more evenly across the two classrooms. I couldn't believe my ears. Mrs. Santine, a superior teacher, was given no credit for her skills in classroom management. If her class was better, it had to be because her kids were easier. This is from a so-called educational leader, who didn't even recognize the difference.

In a sense, all teachers *are* equal, in that they are all at the bottom of the educational food chain. Teachers are on a flat organizational scale, just as teaching is a flat career. Without hierarchy there is no status, and without status there are no distinctions. Making distinctions offends egalitarian sensibilities, but distinctions are necessary in order for humans to make sense of their social landscape. Distinctions guide us through the practices and institutions of our society. In a world without status, we are without a compass.

The Pod at the Devotion School was initiated by Alex Whitman, a reconstructed hippie with a charismatic and intense personality who pulled together a group of teachers over beer and pretzels for about two hours every Friday afternoon. We discussed teaching, schools, families, and just about everything else. Mostly, though, it was about education and how to improve schools. We talked about our practice. Products of the seventies, we saw ourselves as change agents, combining feminism, social revolution, and the notion that we could effect real change in the system. It felt good, as I remember, just talking to other teachers. It was liberating and wonderful—and terribly exclusive and elitist.

We thought we were really cool and very hip, and when teachers we didn't like wanted to be included in the group, we employed various subversive strategies to keep them out. Betty M., for example, a married third grade teacher, wanted to join, and I remember we didn't want her in the group because during the school day she would leave school to sneak down the street to rendezvous with her boyfriend, a Buick salesman, and as liberated as we thought we were, we used that as a rationale for keeping her out. For other teachers, we found other excuses. This created undercurrents of resentment among many teachers, which we were too self-involved to notice, or pay attention to. The Pod, bent on self-actualization, imbued each of us with the feeling that we were going to make real changes in the system. We were riding the groundswell of seventies school reform that manifested itself in the now infamous "alternative schools" and "open classrooms," which aimed at tearing down the barriers between classroom teachers. It was a serious attempt to improve the practice of teaching by bringing teachers together in a forum for collaboration, discussion, and the sharing of methods and ideas. But the movement ran out of steam: the deeply embedded school culture defeated this wave of reform as it has defeated all others before and since.

The Pod lasted about five years before it came to a sad end, partly as a result of school culture and partly because of our own hubris and stupidity. We were the young turks, and with the attitude typical of those who believe they are the holders of a special truth, we ignored the warning signs that we were arousing resentment among the rest of the Devotion teachers. We were committed to breaking down walls, we told ourselves, and indeed we were, among a select group. But in the process we had built an impenetrable wall around an enclave of well-meaning but self-absorbed snobs, insensitive to the need to create an open and accessible group in the midst of a diverse faculty.

Ironically, it fell apart because our principal thought we were engaged in something so exciting that he wanted the rest of the teachers in the school to learn about, and possibly emulate, our model. Jerry Kaplan, the principal, had a simple philosophy: hire the best teachers you can, and stay out of their way. That policy of noninterference gave teachers at Devotion unusual autonomy and created the laissez-faire environment in which the Pod was allowed to flourish. Teachers at Devotion genuinely loved Jerry, and he loved us back.

But Jerry made a mistake. His enthusiasm for a group of teachers who on their own initiative had formed a coterie to promulgate a progressive agenda of education reform struck pride in his paternal principal's heart. So it came as a shock to him, and to the rest of us when, at a general meeting of all the Devotion teachers, Jerry's enthusiasm for the Pod elicited nothing but hurt and angry responses from those teachers who were bold enough to speak out. Teachers complained bitterly, some with shaking voices and tears in their eyes, about being snubbed, shut out, or just ignored. When Jerry made the mistake of telling teachers how exceptional he thought the Pod was, he merely increased resentment against it. Jerry didn't realize that we were viewed as the golden favorites of the principal, and when those feelings came out, it put a damper on our enthusiasm to continue. It wasn't long before the Pod dwindled away. It just dissolved.

The Pod, formed by teachers who desperately felt the need to grow professionally beyond the confines of their classrooms, without giving up teaching, and who had few opportunities for discourse among their peers, was doomed by the culture of the school.

—Kitty

Common sense alone discredits the notion of equality among teachers, given that all parents, and teachers as well, understand that there are exceptional teachers who deserve the highest rewards and incompetent teachers who shouldn't be allowed inside a classroom. That neither of these happens is symptomatic of other factors contributing to teacher isolation: poor supervision, no mentoring, and practically no accountability.

Professions such as medicine and law, to borrow yet again from those examples, require novices to undergo long periods of internship, mentoring, supervision, performance reviews, and gateways to the next level of a hierarchy intended to reward achievement and screen out the least competent. Along the way mechanisms allow the novice to receive assistance, hone skills, and acquire knowledge. The same is not true of teaching, where the novice flies pretty much solo from day one. Often she faces a classroom full of the most difficult children, who have been dumped on her because no one else wants to take them and she lacks the power to negotiate or resist. It's sink or swim. The reasons teachers give for leaving—doubts about their ability to achieve success, absence of growth opportunities, conflicts with colleagues or administrators, failures of classroom management, lack of support—are directly attributable to the norm of isolation.

Their jobs play out in a virtual vacuum: teachers receive no feedback and have no benchmarks against which to measure their own performance. Most of the time they simply don't know how well or how poorly they are doing. They receive no meaningful assessments of their skills and accomplishments, and no guidance for growth and development. The inadequacies of physicians or attorneys become apparent as their performance is subjected to scrutiny. Teaching, on the other hand, is a vocation that—barring certain extremes—shields incompetence and inhibits excellence.

In the culture of schools, isolation and egalitarianism combine to form a tyranny of self-censorship and suppression. This can be observed even in the conversations that teachers have among themselves. Even though the culture in effect constrains conversations regarding instructional practices, we do not mean to suggest that teachers do not enjoy satisfying social relationships. Many socialize with each other outside school. Commonly, however, their conversations, in and out of school, deal with "safe" subjects, such as school politics, gripes, the personalities and family backgrounds of students and parents, home life, and the world outside school.

> Carolyn, a first-year teacher in the school where I was teaching, used to come into the teachers' room and share her classroom experiences with us. She would talk about what she was trying—things she had learned and was having success with in her classroom. When she left the room, all the teachers would roll their eyes and talk about her. I had been teaching for several years and I had befriended Carolyn, and I felt like a mentor to her and felt bad for Carolyn and wanted her to be liked, and to feel accepted. So one day I took her aside and warned her not to tell those stories any more because they were alienating her from the other teachers. Well, of course, she stopped coming to the teachers' room and telling her stories. About a year later I went to a teachers' workshop given by an education consultant, and we were talking about school culture and how it affects our relationships with other teachers. I suddenly realized, when I recounted my experience with Carolyn, what a terrible thing I had done to her. What we all do to each other. I broke down into tears right there in the class.
>
> —Rosalind, a third grade teacher in Attleboro, Massachusetts

The research on the isolation of teachers and the culture of schools is heavy with stories that mirror the experience of Rosalind and Carolyn. It is research that teachers themselves almost never read.

Teachers Are Kept at the Bottom of the Power Structure

American schools embody a structure and culture that denies teachers decision-making power. Decisions that directly affect a teacher's work—textbooks and curriculum, assessment, scheduling, class placement, assignment of specialists, allocation of budgets and materials—these are made by "experts" at higher levels of the school bureaucracy.

In 1759, John Harrison, a self-taught English carpenter, invented the first marine chronometer for the accurate measurement of longitude, a monumental achievement in the history of navigation. Yet it took him twelve years to be awarded the £20,000 prize offered by the British government, because the Admiralty refused to believe that an instrument invented by someone not in the officer class could actually work. Thus it is with the education establishment, which routinely refuses to believe that teachers could have anything meaningful to say about education—and with the world at large, which cannot imagine that a teacher could have anything meaningful to say about anything.

In most professions, practitioners instruct students who are coming into the profession. A lawyer I know gets on a train to New Haven every Tuesday afternoon to teach a course in constitutional law at Yale. There is the appearance, at least, of a seamless continuum between practice and theory, one that assumes mutual respect.

In contrast, public schools and universities have endured a not altogether close relationship that often borders on the antagonistic. There are several reasons for this. To begin with, the field of education is hierarchical, with universities and college professors occupying the higher rungs of power and prestige and public schools and classroom teachers occupying the bottom. Think of a ladder that begins with the kindergarten teacher, rises "upward" through high school, and continues through the undergraduate and finally the graduate schools. It may not be logical, since it is certainly no easier to teach reading to a first grader than it is to teach curriculum development to a graduate student—in fact, the first may even be more difficult and complex—but that's the way it is. The prejudice persists. The older the student, the greater the prestige of his or her teacher. Universities think of themselves as "above" the public schools, and treat public school teachers and principals with disdain.

A true story: February 1986. The Palmer House hotel in Chicago, site of the AACTE conference.[11] Kitty and I were invited to make a presentation at the conference and were taking the elevator from our floor down to the ballroom, where the plenary session was to be held. An academic-looking, professorial-type guy got into the elevator. We could tell from the name tag on his tweed jacket that he was from a large midwestern university and that he was headed for the conference, just as we were. We offered a polite hello. He glanced at our badges, which identified us as fourth grade teachers at a public school. "You're teachers!" he exclaimed, as if having discovered a pair of undercover spies. Obviously, the idea of teachers appearing at a conference having to do with the *education* of teachers was too outlandish a concept for him to comprehend. We could have been from Mars. "What are *you* doing here?" he blurted out. Then, realizing what that must have sounded like, he followed his foot-in-mouth remark with "I mean, . . . but . . . who *are* you?" A moment of dead silence. He looked at the two of us. The unfortunate professor was so anxious to escape from his embarrassment that he got off at the next stop. As the doors closed behind him, we broke into laughter. "Wait till he finds out we're presenting!"
—Vivian

Schools and universities represent different philosophical approaches. University instructors usually deal with the theoretical, classroom teachers with the practical. We've heard university professors talk about "those teachers" who say they want to reform their practice without actually doing anything to keep pace with advancements in education reform. From our perspective, it was university folks who always wanted to "fix" a school without having a clue about how teachers in classrooms really work. A student teacher comes into the classroom to begin practice teaching, having been steeped in the university dogma that veteran classroom teachers are all burned out and you can't learn anything from them. Then the student hears from the classroom teacher that what is taught in university classes is all pie in the sky—ivory-tower talk that has no bearing on the real world. The consequence has always been a lack of communication and respect between the two camps, a self-canceling effect that ultimately results in the graduation of student teachers who are less well prepared to enter the classroom than they should be. Now, wouldn't it make more sense for universities to team up with principals and classroom teachers, the ones who, with sleeves rolled up, carry out the real job of teaching children in the trenches of public education? Imagine if they became partners in melding the theoretical with the practical and actually *collaborated* in the process of teacher development!

The egalitarian nature of teaching is an impediment to teachers' assuming leadership and is thus a handy device for keeping teachers in their place through peer pressure. It is deftly exploited by principals and administrators to dampen initiative and prevent teachers from coalescing around issues affecting policy and the broader purview of education outside the classroom. It is inside the classroom, therefore, that teachers silently exert what little power they have—by resisting change.

The current teaching model—one teacher in a single classroom, doing the same work on the first day of the job as on the last—no longer adequately serves the needs of a radically transformed society. First and foremost we must recognize that one of the most serious obstacles to education reform is the culture of the school; and that culture cannot change until the job of teaching is reconfigured to reflect the reality of how people work and learn in today's world. Successful education reform depends on transforming teaching from an isolated, freelance culture in which mediocrity is the accepted norm, into an open, collaborative culture that fosters professional excellence and accountability.

As the struggle to improve public education enters the public consciousness, many educators are making significant contributions toward developing solutions to the deepening crisis in public education. Some of them are doing a remarkable job of injecting new ideas into a system creaky with age and highly resistant to change. In the end, however, their efforts will manage to achieve only modest and short-lived results. In the words of noted educators David Tyack and Larry Cuban, the history of education reform in America can be described as "tinkering toward utopia."[12] After more than a century of tinkering, we must accept the inescapable fact: *There will be no meaningful, lasting education reform unless we first transform the practice of teaching itself.*

Most people readily acknowledge that the continued existence of a healthy democratic state is dependent on a strong system of education for its citizens. That means that teaching is one of the most important jobs in our society. Teachers play a vital role in children's development. What children learn and experience during their early years shapes their views of themselves and the world and affects their later success or failure in school, at work, and in their personal lives. Students come from a broad range of ethnic, national, and cultural backgrounds. It is in the public schools that the store of American culture, values, and ideals is transmitted. Public schools are the great democratizing force in our society, and it is no exaggeration to state that without public school teachers the whole nature of our republic would be vastly different.

That is why something is very wrong when parents cry out for the highest level of performance from their children's classroom teachers, while at the same time expecting that their smartest and most accomplished children could "do better" than become teachers. Why don't we see this as an untenable contradiction?

In my community, smart young people don't want to be teachers any more. At one time it was an entrance into a profession. But today your parents, people in your church, even your teachers tell you, don't be a teacher. When I told my parents I wanted to be a teacher, they tried to discourage me. "You can be a real success if you major in another field. Go into business." I became a teacher in spite of them. And against the urgings of my friends, too.

—African-American student, Harvard Graduate School of Education

School reform will go nowhere and the quality of public education will be no better than mediocre until a parent is able to say, "My child is going to be a teacher" with the same pride of accomplishment as "My child is going to be a doctor."

This is unlikely to happen until we change the job of the teacher.

Ineffective Leadership Compounds Poor Performance

A teacher's work life is greatly affected by the quality of school leadership, so it is important that we take some time here to understand those forces which have made the principal's job the impossible task it has become in today's schools. As we consider changing the job of the teacher, we must also direct our attention toward changing the job of the principal.

Way back when schools consisted of only one, two, or three rooms, there were no principals. Schools were run by teachers who taught classes, handled the few essential administrative tasks, supervised sports and other activities, and lit the morning fires. Elected members of school boards made decisions about finances, supplies, teacher recruitment and hiring, and daily operations.[13]

With the onset of the Industrial Revolution, burgeoning school populations fueled the growth of new and larger schools. The sudden shift, almost overnight, from small schools to large schools created new problems of school management. A bureaucratic form of school governance, well suited to the rapidly growing schools of the nineteenth century, was established. This new form was developed not only to help manage the growing numbers of teachers and school children, but also to eliminate the graft and political patronage that rode in on the coattails of industrial wealth to plague the developing school systems.

By the late 1800s it had become the practice within this new bureaucracy for one teacher to be designated the headmaster, or principal teacher, whose primary responsibility was to monitor and direct the work of other teachers, as well as to teach. The principal teacher reported to the district superintendent and was first and foremost an instructional leader—that is, one who set educational goals and expectations and then inspired and assisted others to reach them. As schools grew larger and more complex, principal teachers assumed more and more duties. As administrative tasks increased, teaching responsibilities diminished. At the same time, school committees and boards of education, in need of more professional assistance in school management, relinquished many of their administrative responsibilities to the local schools. The idea of a full-time professional administrator rapidly became the norm, and the principal teacher's title was shortened to *principal.* The principal was given authority to make decisions about operating the school, hiring staff, handling finances, and maintaining the school building. The principal no longer taught, yet was still responsible for instructional leadership as well as for the performance of all newly acquired administrative tasks.[14]

By the 1950s principals were, according to their job description at least, responsible for both administrative and instructional leadership. In fact, however, they had by this time become nearly overwhelmed with administrative responsibilities. A 1950s textbook for prospective principals addresses topics including the selection of party treats, the decision whether to erect swings and monkey bars in the school playground, and a discussion on "the Principal as Director and Dispatcher of Traffic." Principals were encouraged to build school spirit by starting the day with a school song, choosing school colors, and having a mascot that represented the school name. To many, this *Leave It to Beaver* image of the elementary school principal represents the golden age of American schools.[15]

Today, the typical principal's responsibilities are likely to include assuring children's physical safety, meeting with the police about drugs and with social workers about a runaway child or suspicion of child abuse, fixing faulty plumbing and heating, making certain the snow is plowed and the roof doesn't leak, controlling parking lot traffic, promoting bicycle safety, supervising school buses and other forms of student transportation, overseeing breakfast and lunch programs and the implementation of the school curriculum—not to mention sex education, health education, and moral education—and guaranteeing programs for gifted children and those with special needs. Principals are held accountable for teacher performance, student achievement on standardized tests, and school morale. Nothing that happens within the boundaries of the school property is considered beyond the purview of the principal.[16]

Because the job of principal covers such a wide range of situations, the work is necessarily characterized by fragmentation, variety, and spurts of frenetic activity. It is unusual for a principal to spend more than a few minutes at one time on a task or be able to complete a major project without interruption. Principals have little control over their time, and most of their days are spent responding to situations, rather than initiating them. According to some studies, 58 percent of a principal's time is devoted to management responsibilities and only 17 percent to instructional leadership. Rarely does the principal visit a classroom for more than a few minutes, and once a teacher is tenured, the number of observations drops precipitously. Teacher evaluations are often based on reputation rather than first-hand supervision. Opportunities for a principal to become immersed in issues surrounding classroom instruction are virtually nonexistent. Paradoxically, principals are hired for their expertise in curriculum and for their record of good teaching, not for their skill in management. Yet it is their management skill that will determine their success or failure.

Principals stand in the center of a busy intersection, mediating between the needs of the school system and the needs of children and their parents; between the school board and the superintendent on one side and teachers and the unions on the other; between academic theory and classroom practice. The breadth of their responsibilities is enormous. They are subject to contradictory demands and must constantly consider competing claims on their time and energy. The principal influences, and is influenced by, all the stakeholders in the educational enterprise—students, parents, employees, community members, policy makers, and of course administrators in the district office.

A principal's job life is dependent on the behavior of people over whom he or she has little control—from "below," as in teacher expectations and demands, or from "above," as in school board dictums and directives. A constant bombardment of new tasks keeps principals off balance. They are always overloaded, either with what they are doing or with what they think they should be doing or with what others demand that they be doing.

Historically, within the job description of the principal, imbalance has always existed between responsibility and authority. A principal has the responsibility of a CEO but the authority of an ineffectual middle manager. Paradoxically, though many in the community believe that, because the job carries with it so much responsibility, the principal must have a lot of power, principals themselves in fact often feel powerless.

Principals believe they have responsibility for everything and control over nothing. They are presented with a curriculum they did not choose and may not agree with. They are presented with a faculty they can do little to shape. A few principals with political clout have some say in hiring, but their power to fire even the most incompetent teacher is almost nonexistent. As a result, a practice known in some places as "pass the trash" has arisen, a scheme in which teachers, unions, and principals are all complicit. Unable to fire a problem teacher, a principal invites him or her to transfer to another school and provides a good reference, thereby sticking another principal in the system with this teacher's inadequacies. It will be a year or two before the victimized principal can then pass that teacher on to another principal. In a school system the size of Boston's, for example, this game could (theoretically) last seventy-five years for an elementary school teacher. It is a custom practiced most successfully in larger urban school systems, and it has national currency. Lacking better strategies, principals exert what little control they have over teaching quality.

There's no hotter seat in all of education than the principal's, nor one more closely examined by professional researchers who, after twenty years of study, agree that, by gosh, principals can make a difference in school improvement and student achievement. Overwhelmingly, the data point to a need for instructional leadership from principals who pay close attention to curriculum and teaching. The potential power of the school principal has been rediscovered; yet the voice of the principal, like the voice of the teacher, is not heard in the swirling debates about education.

A study at the University of Maryland found that principals of the better schools (meaning, where student achievement is measurably higher) round up their own extra resources, track student achievement, recruit good teachers, and demand high quality teaching.[17] Principals of less successful schools function more as middle managers and have lower expectations for teachers. Strangely, principals are neither trained nor rewarded for instructional leadership. The principalship has strayed so far from its original mission that instructional leadership receives little attention in the graduate schools charged with educating principals. The focus is on management and, more and more, on legal issues. Running a school smoothly is the way to receive high marks from central office administrators and is easier than overhauling teaching and learning. Policy makers, blithely ignoring the abundant research on school leadership, have paid little attention to school administration during the current education reform movement.

In education, administration has come to mean not the management of instruction, but the management of the structures and processes surrounding instruction. The administrative structure of schools is designed to buffer the instructional core, not to disturb it, and least of all to improve it. Direct involvement in instruction is among the activities administrators of any kind perform at any level least frequently. Principals sometimes proclaim with pride their success in achieving their primary goal—protecting "their" teachers from outside demands. The institutional structure does not promote, or select for, knowledge and skill related to instructional leadership.

When asked, principals report that they would like to be instructional leaders who work closely with teachers, children, and the curriculum; however, the job, as it is currently structured, provides little to support them in that role. Many principals cite "having a strong vision" as the most important characteristic for a principal. Yet the typical career path from teacher to principal makes this unlikely. Having "vision" is not part of a teacher's job (although we would argue that it ought to be), and expecting a principal, after years of teaching, suddenly to acquire this trait is highly unrealistic.

Principals, recruited almost exclusively from the ranks of teachers, come to their jobs well versed in the norms, values, predispositions, and routines of the traditional school organization—in effect, well socialized.[18] We need to ask why it is taken for granted that a principal must have years of teaching experience. Having spent the first part of a career learning how to interact with children would not seem a useful prerequisite for a job whose main function is working with adults. It's the same old story of the brilliant salesperson elevated to sales manager, who no longer sells and is deficient as a manager.

Excellent teachers often make dismal principals. It is possible that a principal who was trained in another field of administration would find the school culture impenetrable. Because a principal is already acculturated, though, thinking outside the box is extremely difficult, if not impossible.

Now here's some more bad news. There aren't enough principals to go around, and current projections point toward a severe shortage in the next decade. Half the school districts surveyed in a national study reported a shortage of qualified candidates for vacancies, in all types of schools, rural, suburban, and urban.[19] A number of causes have been cited, including the top three: compensation that is considered inadequate for the responsibilities of the position, the impossible demands of the job, and the long hours required. Of course, there is a more obvious reason—fewer college graduates are going into teaching; and as the number of qualified teachers decreases, so does the pool of those who would consider becoming principals.

Today's schools desperately need the leadership good principals can provide, but there's little chance they're going to get it any time soon—that is, unless we consider how to make it possible for principals to work more closely with teachers on the problems of education, while handing over the non-education-related tasks of management to specially trained assistants.

5 Band-Aids and Boondoggles: The Myths and Realities of "Education Reform"

For every complicated problem there is a solution that is short, simple, and wrong.—H. L. Mencken

We have argued that the most critical mission of education reform is the transformation of the teaching profession. We shall now attempt to convince a rightly skeptical audience that one systemic reform—the Millennium School—could change the nature of schools and schooling in America for the better. Teachers and teaching will be so vastly improved by the Millennium School, we maintain, that the result will be a demonstrably better system of education benefiting not only teachers but children and parents as well. To see clearly why this reform—actually a comprehensive program of integrated reforms—would actually work, it is necessary to take a critical look at the most pervasive of the current so-called reforms and understand where and how they fail. They resemble flawed pieces of a puzzle that just doesn't fit together.

"For over a century," say David Tyack and Larry Cuban, "citizens have sought to perfect the future by debating how to improve the young through education. Actual reforms in schools have rarely matched such aspirations, however."[1]

Why have education reforms so seldom achieved their intended aims over the long term, and why have measurable gains proven so elusive? Change is not synonymous with progress, even though some changes have been deep and long-lasting, for better and for worse.

Kindergarten, for example, was first introduced in Boston in 1860 by education reformer Elizabeth Peabody, not as part of the public schools but as an "antidote" to them. Peabody felt that the public schools were too rigid and that their curricula were not appropriate to the education of young children, who were more likely to benefit, she believed, from participation in organized games, music, artwork, gymnastics, gardening, and social interaction. Kindergartens became immensely popular, and a movement to include them as part of the public schools became widespread. A hundred years later, more than 60 percent of all five-year-olds were enrolled in a public school kindergarten.[2] Over time, kindergartens began to mimic first grade, but with smaller people. The original aim of kindergarten, to adapt education to the needs of young children, changed. Now the aim was to adapt young children to the needs of schooling. The reform was intended to change the school; instead, school changed the reform— not an unusual outcome of school reform.

The notion of the junior high school also received its impetus from reformers highly critical of the public school system. At the beginning of the twentieth century, schooling was usually delivered through eight elementary school grades and four high school grades. The attrition rate, however, was extremely high. About 90 percent of students never made it all the way through to graduation from high school. Education reformers blamed the narrow academic curriculum and the rigidity of the school system and proposed a completely new formula for educating students that would include the insertion of a "junior high school" after sixth grade and the replacement of grades seven to eight (or nine). The junior high would offer new subjects, new methods of teaching appropriate to that restricted age group (the concept of adolescence had just been discovered), and an opportunity for students to sort out whether they wished to continue their academic career or select a vocational track instead. Several interest groups jumped on the junior high school bandwagon: social investigators who were frustrated with past attempts to rectify the high dropout rate; developmental psychologists pushing for ways to adapt schooling to the particular needs of adolescents—individual differences compounded by acceleration in physical growth; curriculum reformers who envisioned the realization of the junior high school as a means by which to restructure the entire school system; and textbook publishers who saw a gold mine of new sales opportunities opening up before their eyes. Not all educators were enthusiastic, though. Some warned that, without a carefully thought-out program of curriculum and teaching, the junior high school would fail to live up to its promise and instead create more problems than it solved. That is indeed what happened. It is easier to copy an existing institution than to create a new one; so instead of establishing a brand-new model which met the criteria designed to serve this intermediate group of young people, the junior high school (now often called a middle school) fell into the trap of emulating the familiar high school, and it failed to achieve its aims. Over time, retention rates in high schools did rise, but for reasons unrelated to the junior high school—compulsory education, for one. Again, the school changed the reform, rather than the other way around.[3]

We present these examples to illustrate that school reform is not a novel concept but an ongoing process. It has been taking place since the first student entered the first classroom, and it is unlikely that Americans will stop tinkering with their system to correct what they believe to be its flaws. It is our contention, however, that much of today's tinkering consists of Band-Aids and boondoggles that do far more harm than good and solve none of the basic problems they were intended to correct. Heretofore, the solutions have been too narrow in focus. Reformers have failed to recognize the underlying causes of dysfunction, which are interdependent and self-perpetuating. Public education has become a closed-loop system of dysfunction.

More Testing

In his 1997 State of the Union Address, President Bill Clinton called for "a national crusade for education standards" and proposed a set of new Voluntary National Tests that would "test every fourth grader in reading and every eighth grader in math to make sure these standards are met."[4]

In his first week in office, President George W. Bush called for the testing of all public school students in grades 3 through 8. "States should test each student each year. Without yearly testing, we don't know who is falling behind and who needs help."[5] To follow up on his pledge, the president soon engineered into law a far-reaching $26-billion education bill called the No Child Left Behind Act of 2001. It promises, among other things, to spend billions of dollars (and to demand that states also spend billions) on more testing, testing, testing. "We've spent billions of dollars, with lousy results. Now it's time to spend billions of dollars and get good results," said the president.[6] The National Association of State Boards of Education estimated that states would need to spend as much as $7 billion over the next seven years to develop, administer, and score the new tests.[7]

Presidents, it seems, are not immune to the siren call of America's latest panic-driven fad, which insists that if something is good (for example, testing) then more is even better.

> The public is often impatient for change, and it is the quick fix embodied in intensification policy that invariably focuses on easy solutions, a mentality that gives little weight to the process by which change occurs.[8]

America's obsession with testing has become a national madness, a blind flight from rational thought and behavior. Testing is a pervasive drug so seductive that we find it increasingly difficult to just say no, no matter how costly and counterproductive it may prove to be. When tests fail to produce the anticipated cure, we alter the dosage by giving them more often or making them either easier or harder to take. It seems to make no difference that the new law will allocate billions of dollars for a strategy that has never been shown to have a positive effect on children's learning and intellectual growth. Large-scale testing merely serves to rob students of precious hours of classroom instruction while enriching the large testing companies, which can now look forward to rapid growth in the current $50-million testing market.[9] We're hooked on tests.

Tests, of course, have always played a role in helping teachers assess how much material individual students have remembered, and how far students have progressed since the last time a test was administered. We need tests, and it would be both foolish and irresponsible to suggest that we can do without them. But testing is only one assessment tool, and it should be used only where appropriate. Not all tests are appropriate for all situations. You don't use a sledgehammer in place of a screwdriver. High-stakes testing, as it is now being called—a single test that determines a student's placement, promotion, or graduation—has assumed such a critical role in the politics of education policy that many parents, teachers, and educators are becoming deeply concerned about its effects on the educational process.

American students are being tested more often now than ever before in our history and far more than other students elsewhere in the world. In Japan, for example, a country widely admired for the ability of its education system to produce outstanding test takers, standardized testing does not start until the end of sixth grade. Massive amounts of testing have not helped, nor can it ever help, to improve the quality of education. "You can't fatten cattle by weighing them more often," observed a savvy rancher. To state it another way, taking your temperature does not lower your fever.

Test-based reform strategies have enjoyed wide acceptance across the political spectrum—at least in theory—for two reasons. First, who could possibly be against "high standards?" Second, most Americans believe in the accuracy and fairness of judging students by what [President

Clinton] has called "good tests." But what constitutes a good test? How do we know a test is good—that it really measures what it is supposed to measure? And, equally important, how do we know that the test and its results are being used properly by teachers and administrators who have the power to make important decisions about individual children?[10]

Tests are not always "good." As a matter of fact, they are often woefully imperfect. Nationwide, the sudden rush by states to use testing as a strategy for achieving "accountability" and "raising academic standards" has caught the multibillion-dollar testing industry unprepared. As more and more states create and institute statewide tests, testing companies scramble to hire scorers to grade them. Most are part-time workers who receive little or no training before being thrown onto the scoring assembly line. Small mistakes, multiplied by computers, snowball into nightmares. A simple keying error made by NCS Pearson, the nation's largest test scorer, assigned 47,000 Minnesota students lower scores than they deserved. A mistake on a multiple-choice exam given in Arizona significantly lowered scores for 12,000 students. In 1997, a mistake made by a small testing company denied $2 million in achievement awards to deserving Kentucky schools. In 1999, almost 9,000 New York City students were mistakenly assigned to summer school because of a flawed test. It was six months before the error was detected.[11] When tests are poorly designed, otherwise flawed, or incorrectly scored, students suffer. When the stakes are high, students suffer badly. Many fail to graduate, cannot enter college, or lose out on scholarships. Teachers and schools suffer as well, for they often take the blame for poor student performance.

The theory is that testing enforces accountability and high standards for all. How can anyone believe, though, that one high-stakes test can measure the academic progress of any student? Multiple indicators must be employed. The belief that if we set standards high enough, students will miraculously attain higher levels of academic achievement is delusional. What happens when theory bangs up against reality and the failure rates on statewide tests reach appalling levels? States have taken a hard line regarding accountability, but as deadlines approach for denying students diplomas, state administrators will blink. Tough talk gives way to backpedaling. According to Monty Neill, executive director of FairTest, a group based in Cambridge, Massachusetts, "It appears that failure rates on these tests are so high that they are literally politically untenable."[12]

Each state has its own backpedaling strategies. In Alaska, after seeing the high failure rate on a test required for high school graduation, Governor Tony Knowles urged the legislature to delay the high-stakes exam for four years. Only 8 percent of children in special education passed the test, so the governor suggested a different approach for SPED students. The current solution: add $16 million to the education budget.[13]

When it became evident that too many fourth graders would not move on to the next grade, Ohio lawmakers nullified a requirement that would have compelled all fourth graders to score at the "proficient" level in reading before going on to fifth grade.

Disappointing test results in Wyoming led to the creation of three different diplomas: advanced, proficient, and individualized. California decided to delete some of the most difficult math questions on its statewide exam and shorten the test by as much as an hour. In Arizona, where 88 percent of the sophomores failed the math portion of the 1999 statewide test, education officials acknowledged that the linkage is inadequate between the state's math standards and what teachers are teaching in the classroom. "They're high-quality standards," says state representative John Huppenthal, "but they just present an enormous political problem—essentially a train wreck—in which children who have been accepted to quality universities can't get out of high school."[14]

The people who work most closely with kids are those most likely to understand how harmful standardized testing is. . . . Support for such tests seems to grow as you move further from the students, going from teacher to principal to central office administrator to school board member to state board member, state legislator, and governor. Those for whom classroom visits are occasional photo opportunities are most likely to be big fans of testing and to offer self-congratulatory sound bites about the need for "tougher standards" and "accountability."[15]

Pressure to increase test scores comes from the top down. School boards put pressure on superintendents, who put pressure on principals, who put pressure on teachers, who, of course, put pressure on students, who don't need any more pressure. Stakes for success or failure are high. Schools may be judged according to the average scores of their students schoolwide. High schoolwide scores may attract public praise and financial rewards; low scores may bring public reproach or heavy sanctions. For individual students, high scores may merit a special diploma attesting to exceptional academic accomplishment; low scores may result in students' being held back in grade or denied a high school diploma.[16] With so much riding on test scores, the pressure, and the atmosphere of fear and apprehension it creates can be harmful to the integrity of the system. The Massachusetts Department of Education has documented violations of test rules in at least nineteen Massachusetts schools. In New York City dozens of teachers and principals were found to have supplied students with correct answers on standardized reading and math tests. The Michigan Senate Education Committee has called for an investigation of alleged cheating on a statewide test taken at seventy-one schools. Similar scandals have been uncovered in Connecticut, Texas, Nevada, California, Maryland, Ohio, Florida, and Kentucky.

Statewide testing not only burdens teachers with test-performance pressures, it also creates insoluble quandaries about how to teach. Virtually every state administers performance tests that all children in selected grades must take. That city kids must take additional tests, such as the Stanford 9, merely compounds the inequities that exist between children in urban districts and their more affluent suburban neighbors. One reason given for administering the extra exams is that the norms for scoring them are developed on the basis of test data from urban children—by contrast with other tests, which use norms developed from a broader population. As a consequence, the very children who need more hours of instruction have learning time siphoned off for more testing. But that's not the worst of it. Rarely is the Stanford 9 aligned with the specially designed statewide tests. In Massachusetts, for example, the Stanford 9, given in urban districts in the second grade, requires children to know the borrowing and carrying algorithm—a highly specific way of approaching math problems; however, the Massachusetts Comprehensive Assessment System (MCAS) test given to all fourth graders requires that children know how to solve math problems in several different ways and also to write about their methods. Now, what is the second grade teacher supposed to do, knowing that her students are going to take the Stanford 9 with its emphasis on one method but then in the fourth grade are destined to take the MCAS, for which they will be expected to know another method? She has to teach to the test, of course, but which one? It is not surprising, then, that a ten-state study revealed little overlap between state standards and what teachers in the state say they are teaching.[17]

In Massachusetts 33 percent of tenth graders failed the English section of MCAS in 1999, and 56 percent failed the math. The tests (which in 1999 took seventeen hours—longer than the Massachusetts bar exam) are so controversial that the Massachusetts Teachers Association spent $600,000 on a public relations campaign to discredit what it calls the "one-size fits-all, high-stakes, do-or-die MCAS tests." At the same time, state officials spent $1.5 million on a public relations campaign of their own to boost public support.[18] That's $2.1 million allocated not for improving the test, helping students in trouble, or supporting teachers but for propagandizing an already wary public.

Faint glimmers of rationality remain, accompanied by a resistance to high-stakes testing. In the spring of 2000 Senator Paul Wellstone of Minnesota and Representative Robert Scott of Virginia filed legislation in the Senate and House that would bar states and districts that receive federal education aid from using test scores as the "sole determinant" in decisions about "the retention, graduation, tracking, or within-class ability grouping of an individual student."[19] Although the proposed legislation was given little chance of passage, it is a clear indication of the public's dissatisfaction with high-stakes testing. Like battle-scarred warriors surveying the carnage on a battlefield where there are no winners, education officials around the country are considering what could have been done better and are rethinking the objectives and strategies of statewide testing. The Wellstone-Scott bill is enormously complex (it is more than a thousand pages thick), and it mandates that the federal government pour huge amounts of money into the states in addition to the money contributed by the states themselves. Its passage would, we fear, make it all the more difficult for rational thinkers to prevail.

As we pointed out earlier, high-stakes testing is the errant child of the standards-based reform movement in public education. Standards-based reform calls for establishing high academic standards and expectations for all students, rigorous (but not high-stakes) tests that measure whether students are meeting those standards, and systems of accountability that provide incentives and rewards to help students reach those standards.

What we don't know about academic achievement is a morass, yet we do know this for a fact: the two most important indicators of student success are the child's socioeconomic status and the mother's level of schooling.[20] We could realize significantly better results simply by taking a large portion of the hundreds of millions of dollars now wasted on high-stakes testing and using it to lift children out of poverty and mothers into further education. Of course, that is unlikely to happen.

We both support the aims and objectives of this reform strategy and believe in national standards for academic achievement, as well as fair and accurate measurement. But high-stakes testing must be eliminated from the equation of standards-based education. It is appropriate and necessary to establish high standards and then to assess academic achievement on the basis of those standards; however, it is not only unrealistic but just plain wrong to hold students accountable before teachers are prepared to teach to those standards. Until then, statewide testing will not be an integral component of sensible education reform but an expensive, damaging, and counterproductive boondoggle.

Smaller Classes

Isn't it a foregone conclusion that if you reduce the number of kids in a class, academic achievement will automatically go up? Unfortunately, it just isn't that simple. For a long time there was little reliable research to demonstrate conclusively that lowering class size would have an effect on student achievement, despite the millions of dollars spent on study after study. Year after year, flaws were found in the research. Mountains of statistics built up, but no general agreement on the results could be reached.

That was before the now-famous Tennessee STAR (Student-Teacher Achievement Ratio) study, begun in the mid-1980s, which is now generally acknowledged as the benchmark everybody was waiting for. Its various phases took place over fourteen years, cost $12 million, and tracked about 11,600 students in seventy-nine Tennessee schools. It is famous for having shown that, at least in the controlled conditions of this study, students in kindergarten through third grade who were taught in classes of thirteen to seventeen students outperformed students in standard-size classes of twenty-two to twenty-five. Not only that, but when they reached fourth, sixth, and eighth grades, students from the smaller classes were six to fourteen months ahead of their peers elsewhere in math, reading, and science. The

STAR study also showed that such students were likelier to complete more advanced math and English courses, to finish high school, to graduate on time, and to graduate with honors.[21]

Here, at last, was something for advocates of small class size to cheer about. The Tennessee STAR study seemed to prove in dramatic fashion that smaller class sizes can bring about improved academic achievement. We emphasize the word *can* because, as many states have since discovered to their dismay, the stellar results of the STAR project are not automatically achievable in all schools. Why? Let's look at what Tennessee had, which so few other states enjoy today. In the mid-1980s Tennessee had an abundance of available certified, qualified teachers in the workforce. When the state needed to acquire the additional teachers necessary to teach the extra classes, it simply hired them. All new hires were state certified and qualified to teach in their assigned grades. Tennessee schools also had enough available classroom space. They had no need to cannibalize art and music rooms or libraries or gymnasiums or to put kids in trailers in parking lots or playgrounds. These factors have been largely ignored by other states looking at Tennessee's results and saying, "Hey, we could do that here!"

No state better illustrates the pitfalls of a misguided policy initiative than California, with its CSR (class size reduction) program. In 1996 Governor Pete Wilson faced a set of huge and growing problems in the state's sprawling education system. Per-pupil spending was fortieth in the country. Population was swelling at a time when many elementary school classes already contained thirty-five students or more. Test scores, particularly in urban schools, lagged behind the national averages. Some school districts, most notably the Los Angeles Unified School District, the second largest in the country, were in chaos. Still, on the bright side, the expanding economy had put surplus dollars into the state treasury. The governor, inspired by the results of Tennessee's STAR project, decided to use the money ($1.5

billion over three years) to reduce class sizes. Unfortunately, implementation of the Class Size Reduction Act in the school years 1997–98 and 1998–99 created a number of serious problems.[22]

The first was the equal but unfair distribution of resources. The state board of education decided on the number twenty (not thirteen to seventeen as in Tennessee) to define small class size and allocated $650 (since raised to $800) per pupil for each classroom in a district that reached that target.[23] Funding was offered across the board, regardless of the socioeconomic makeup of the district. This amount did not cover the actual cost per pupil, so individual school districts had to make up the additional dollars themselves, something that affluent suburban districts were able to do more easily than poorer urban districts. Suburban schools also had more space available for extra classrooms, and it was easier for them to put additional trailer classrooms on adjacent land. Land-poor urban schools had to give up parking lots or playgrounds—or take over music rooms or art rooms or gymnasiums and then cut back on those programs.

The second problem was the teacher shortage, already notorious in California. The need to hire an additional 28,000 teachers over two years exacerbated the existing shortage in several ways. More unqualified teachers were hired on waivers. The wealthier districts raised salaries or created additional recruitment incentives to lure qualified teachers away from urban schools. The vacuum also sucked in people from day care centers and private schools, creating additional statewide shortages of teachers and child-care workers in areas other than public education.

The cost of the California CSR experiment is now approaching $4 billion, and it is too soon to gauge its results. Most research findings have focused on the problems the districts have had in putting the program in place. Some observers say the shortage of qualified teachers together with the lack of adequate classroom space have doomed this initiative to failure.[24]

Follow-up studies conducted elsewhere have yielded rather conclusive confirmation that in inner-city schools, in the lowest grades (kindergarten through third grade), smaller class sizes can help improve student achievement. For all others, however, there is no evidence whatsoever that simply reducing class size (in the absence of other changes, such as improved teaching skills) has any statistically significant effect. Despite the lack of evidence, the goal of achieving smaller class sizes regardless of cost has become one of the mantras of the nation's school-improvement agenda. Simply reducing the size of a class may not be enough, though. The real payoff appears to come only when teachers shift their practices to take advantage of smaller class size. Specifically, pupils perform at higher levels when teachers use one-to-one contact to focus on strengthening basic skills, provide frequent feedback, and ask children to discuss and demonstrate what they know. This usually doesn't happen without additional teacher training.

> Class size reduction is popular because it's a simple, easy program to communicate to state legislators. . . . Existing evidence indicates that achievement for the typical student will be unaffected by instituting the types of class size reductions that have been recently proposed or undertaken. The most noticeable feature of policies to reduce overall class sizes will be a dramatic increase in the costs of schooling, an increase unaccompanied by achievement gains. It is clear . . . that teacher quality differences are much more important than variations in class size.[25]

What is the bottom line? Simply this: the costs associated with blindly following a class size reduction policy are absolutely staggering, and such a policy is unlikely to bring about significant academic improvement. No research has shown that a student in a small class taught by a poorly trained, underqualified teacher is better off than a student in a larger class led by a top-notch skilled practitioner.

Now, where do you think we should be putting our money?

School Vouchers

Because school "vouchers" are funded through many sources—city and state governments, private donations, foundations, and so forth—the requirements and regulations that govern them are complex enough to defy attempts at simple explanation; however, the basic philosophy behind school vouchers is this: you, as a taxpayer, should have the right to take your per-pupil public education–directed tax dollars and use them to send your child to any (nonpublic) school as you see fit (with certain broad restrictions). In other words, voucher programs are designed by policy makers to make public funds available to defray (if not entirely cover) the costs of attending private schools.

Those who are in favor of vouchers contend that not all children receive the same education in the current public school system and dispute the notion that only public schools can meet the democratic educational aims of the country. Educational programs, they point out, are different in each school district because they are based on the financial resources and priorities of community residents. The proponents come from various arenas but in general tend to fall into one of two camps—minorities who argue quite persuasively that the public schools are failing the minority and urban poor populations in our country, and those on the religious right (of all faiths) who claim their prerogative to use tax dollars to support the education of their children in nonsecular schools. Also generating noise on the pro-voucher side of the debates are those who look on the public schools as a government-run monopoly. "Why should socialism work better for education than for anything else?" asks the economist Milton Friedman, who believes that schools should compete in a "free-market economy."[26]

Let's be honest. Public schools are in trouble all over the country, but schools in poor urban neighborhoods are an unmitigated disaster.

Desperate parents want out—no matter how. Vouchers seem to be a lifeline: why not grasp it? This does not mean that minority leaders speak with a single voice regarding the issue of school vouchers. Bishop Jackson, national president of the Samaritan Project (a creation of the Christian Coalition), echoes many black parents' opinions when he says, "In the past, education was the means for African Americans to overcome the obstacles to success and prosperity. Today the greatest obstacle facing black children in America is the education system itself." On the other side, the NAACP believes that vouchers will destroy the country's public schools and asserts that black teachers and administrators in urban schools regard the idea as anathema.[27]

Those opposed to voucher programs say that vouchers divert resources from already financially strapped school districts, that they subvert the constitutional principle of separation of church and state, and that they have the potential to weaken and undermine our entire public school system and thereby threaten the health of American democracy. They also point out that there is little evidence that students who have been able to take advantage of vouchers do any better academically once they have "escaped" from the public schools. Data measuring the academic performance of students enrolled in voucher programs are hard to come by because unlike public school students, private school pupils are not required to take state-mandated tests.

> The literature on vouchers and academic achievement adds up to an inconsistent gaggle of results that do not offer intelligible guidance to either parents or policymakers . . . [yet] despite the preliminary character and inconsistent outcomes of voucher research, well financed voucher advocates are now sowing confusion by saying that the achievement evidence is clear, systematic and compelling.[28]

Empirical evidence is not sufficiently compelling to justify either strong advocacy or opposition to large-scale voucher programs. In some cases there is simply a paucity of credible evidence. In others, evidence from non-voucher systems is used inappropriately to forecast the impact of large-scale voucher programs.[29]

Those looking to support the notion of vouchers can, however, point to scattered areas of minimal success.

Begun in 1990–91, the longest running voucher initiative in the United States is in Milwaukee, where roughly 8,000 students in ninety-one schools participate.[30] The state of Wisconsin commissioned a study to compare the achievement of students who received vouchers with students of similar socioeconomic background in public schools. In that study, conducted over five years, John Witte of the University of Wisconsin-Madison found no differences in achievement between voucher students and comparable public school students.[31]

Perhaps the largest ongoing study of school voucher programs is that being conducted by the Program on Education Policy and Governance at Harvard University's Kennedy School of Government. This study focuses on low-income students in New York City in grades 2 through 5 who received privately funded vouchers to attend private schools. After one year, it was found that those students scored higher on math and reading tests than a control group of students. Yet gains were modest, around two percentile points (averaged across ethnic groups) in each subject.[32]

On the other side, there is plenty of evidence to show that whatever small success vouchers may have achieved is overshadowed by their immense cost and deleterious effect on the schools whose best students have left. No one can blame parents, rich or poor, for actively seeking the best possible education for their children. Almost always, though, it is the parents and students who are aggressive, savvy, and energetic enough to take advantage of alternative opportunities who leave the schools that need them the most. Parents of school voucher kids tend to be better educated themselves. Voucher programs are in a negative way self-selecting—they take away the students and parents that struggling schools can least afford to lose. Left behind are those who need the most help. Those parents who elect voucher programs are also better off economically than those left behind. They have to be, because vouchers—typically valued between $2,500 and $5,000—often cover only part of the cost of a student's entry into a private school. In New York City, 38 percent of parents who were able to get vouchers could not use them, and in Dayton, Ohio, and Washington, D.C., 47 percent were unable to use their vouchers. Either they could not afford the difference in tuition, or they could not find convenient private schools that would accept them.[33]

Students currently receive vouchers through a variety of programs in a number of large cities, including Milwaukee, Cleveland, Dayton, New York, and New Orleans. Other voucher programs exist in locations in Florida, Ohio, Wisconsin, New Jersey, and Washington, D.C. Some states, such as Arizona, Illinois, Iowa, and Minnesota, provide parents with limited tax credits or deductions to help defray the costs of tuition at a private school.

Vouchers are not universally popular, however. That a majority of Americans are skeptical about vouchers, or strongly opposed to them, is borne out by the fact that voters have rejected all but one of the tuition voucher proposals put on the ballot since the first such vote more than thirty years ago.[34] State legislators who propose voucher programs are in constant battle with state courts, which are increasingly finding vouchers unconstitutional. It is important to keep in mind that publicly funded voucher programs serve fewer than 15,000 students in the United States, a minuscule percentage of the total school population.[35]

Although it is true that a small number of Americans would continue to advocate supporting religious education through tax dollars no matter what the health of public education, most Americans are opposed to the idea, including the majority of church leaders and religious organizations. The strongest reason that school vouchers as an education policy have received any traction at all is the depressing condition of the public schools. If the public schools were in better shape, the issue of school vouchers would disappear into the background.

Vouchers—their promulgation, prevention, study, legislation, and other corollary activities (whole careers are spent on this issue)—consume enormous amounts of time and money. Vouchers are more than a policy subculture, they are an entire industry. It would be difficult to calculate in dollars the total amount being spent on vouchers, but, to judge by all that we have studied and read, the sums must be in the hundreds of millions of dollars—enough, we suspect, to sustain the annual budget of a small third-world country.

Voucher programs are both Band-Aid and boondoggle. They are looked upon as a quick fix, although they are not, and the vast amounts of money being spent for their support on the one hand and on opposition to them on the other would be more productively spent on initiatives such as increasing teachers' salaries and improving teacher training. Those kinds of spending would at least be investments in school improvement rather than contributors to school decline.

Charter Schools

Charter schools are public schools that, using public funds as well as money they may raise on their own, operate independently under a "charter" granted by their state. These schools may be run by groups of parents and teachers, under a supervisory board, or they may be managed by an entrepreneurial for-profit organization answerable to shareholders who seek a return on their investment (more about for-profit school management organizations in the next section). In many states, charters are remarkably easy to obtain and very few applications are denied. Charter schools incorporate both public and private elements. They are publicly funded or supported and publicly accredited and authorized, but they are exempt from some key public constraints. The theory is that, freed of restrictions that their organizers claim are holding back the academic performance of the traditional public school (namely, unions and "bloated bureaucracies"), charter schools will be able to institute innovative programs, teaching methods, and other school reforms that will raise academic achievement and provide a richer educational experience for their students. They may, for example, be free to hire teachers who are not certified or members of a teachers' union and to develop distinctive curricular adaptations. Supervised by state officials and an active board, the theory goes, and freed of the protections provided by the teachers' unions, they will be able to raise the level of accountability.

Minnesota enacted the first charter school law in 1991. Since then policy makers have instituted charter school programs in thirty-six other states and the District of Columbia. The number of charter schools now exceeds 1,700 nationwide, with more than 300,000 students in attendance.[36] The median size of a charter school is under two hundred students, and just over half of charter schools are elementary schools. With the backing of the Clinton administration, Congress allocated hundreds of millions of dollars to encourage the start-up of charter schools, and charter schools continue to enjoy bipartisan support, for they help politicians demonstrate that they are on the reform side of the education issue.

Not everyone is an enthusiastic champion of charter schools, however, and in the highly charged debate each side is eager to prove its point. If you are a supporter of charter schools, you can find several that demonstrate a certain degree of success, and if you are a critic of charter schools, you don't have to look far to find examples of failures so awful they would make you weep.

A few schools have achieved modest improvements in academic performance, but not many. In most instances, academic performance has kept pace with that of surrounding neighborhood schools or fallen below it. In Texas, for example, where more than half of all teachers in charter schools have no form of certification, only 37.9 percent of students in charter schools passed the 1999–2000 statewide TASS exam, as compared with 80 percent of students in other public schools.[37]

The major accomplishment of charter schools has been their ability to provide a safe and nurturing environment (no trivial thing, to be sure), and this achievement has mostly to do with their small size and the involvement of activist parents who invest a great deal of effort to get their kids into a charter school and to keep them there. Parents are, in general, happy with the improved climate offered by charter schools, and waiting lists are long. A strong belief exists among many parents that their children are doing better in their new school. Wherever charter schools have been successful, community involvement—as well as dedicated staff and faculty—have been the key.

The failures, and the reasons for them, are more complex. They have to do with poor planning, fiscal mismanagement, lack of oversight, bad judgment, overambitiousness, and a host of other unanticipated problems, including fraud. Indicted by a grand jury on thirty-one counts of fraud, theft, and the misuse of $179,000 in public funds, the founders of an Arizona charter school declared bankruptcy and closed the school.[38] When a Los Angeles–based charter school failed owing to "fiscal improprieties," California taxpayers lost more than a million dollars, which can never be recovered because California charter law has no provisions for such recovery.[39]

According to some advocates of the charter school model, a critical weakness of traditional public schools is that they have no incentive to improve, because it is impossible to close them down for poor academic performance. Yet even failing public schools, and heaven knows there are plenty, still have classes with students in them. Charter schools that fail, mostly because of financial rather than academic problems, can just close their doors; the schoolchildren are out of luck, left to look for a school that will accept them. Some charter schools have closed overnight, without informing parents, who drive up the next morning to find the doors locked. These are, to be sure, extreme cases, but they demonstrate that where schooling is a market-driven consumable, it will be vulnerable to market forces. In an environment where "only the strong will survive," failure can be devastating.

It is a persistent myth that charter schools, with their autonomy over their own budgets, can be run less expensively than regular public schools. This has not proved to be the case. In California, the extra funding required per pupil for charter schools is running at about $500; in Michigan, $600; in Arizona, $1,000; in Massachusetts, $1,300.[40] This in spite of the fact that charter schools are often "overfunded" because they serve fewer children at risk or with special needs yet receive the same level of funding as other public schools. Furthermore, charter schools, not being bound by union regulations, are free to hire younger or less qualified teachers at lower salaries (and overwork them).

Then why do they need all that extra money? A charter school lacks the infrastructure of an established public school and has to create its own, duplicating in many cases the kinds of equipment, personnel, and services made available by the school district to the regular public school. Of necessity, the charter school must become, in effect, its own district. One charter school in Massachusetts, for example, considered to be among the best in the state, has two hundred students. Running that small school seems to require one headmaster, one executive office manager, one deputy headmaster, three full-time deans, one development associate, two nurses, one psychologist, one occupational therapist, one family services coordinator, one library and media specialist, one high school placement counselor, and one part-time curriculum consultant. All these people are paid, some more than others. A dean's salary is more than $50,000 a year, whereas a beginning teacher can make as little as $24,000. Hence another irony: burdened by the need to duplicate personnel and services ordinarily provided by an existing infrastructure, charter schools end up creating what they had promised to avoid: a bloated bureaucracy, and one in which the teacher—and hence, the student— is again shortchanged.

A word about the above-mentioned job of "curriculum consultant." Driven quite regularly by their directors' egos, charter schools often find themselves being "innovative" in curriculum development. If it's good enough for a regular public school, goes the thinking, it can't be good enough for a charter school. Many excellent and proven math, reading, and science curricula are available off the shelf, but charter schools tend to expend huge amounts of time and money creating new ones. To be fair, charter schools are sometimes required by state laws governing charters to deliver innovative instructional practices and report on their effectiveness—an attempt to encourage fresh thinking and build more accountability into the process. It seldom works that way.

First . . . charter schools are recommended because they are meant to serve as locations for experimentation and innovation. They have generally failed in this regard. The most consistent finding in study after study is that there is virtually no controlled experimentation in charter schools and little innovation. Although some citizens might say they don't care about . . . innovative practices because they just want children to receive a good education . . . in many states the charter laws mandate innovation as well as documentation of improved educational outcomes. If charter directors in these states choose not to innovate, they are taking public funds under false pretenses.

A second concern is that, despite the rhetoric aimed at reducing bureaucracy and getting funds focused on classroom instruction, charter schools have been relatively unsuccessful in this regard. Simply put, charter schools are spending more on administration and less on direct classroom instruction than are other public schools . . . the undeniable issue is that charter advocates have not delivered on their promise to reduce "bloated bureaucracies" and to direct more funds to support classroom activities. The question then becomes, do citizens prefer more money to be spent on administration or on classroom instruction?

A third concern . . . is that charter schools, on average, have a tendency to further segregate students by ethnicity, income level, and special needs . . . charter schools, as a group, seek students who are less costly to educate . . . for-profit schools in particular try to find students who are easy and inexpensive to educate. These pressures are likely to escalate as more investors are drawn into the market. It has been estimated that at least $6 billion in venture capital has been invested in private, for-profit educational firms. Some predict that the assault on public schools by the private sector has just begun and that there will be a series of attempts to increase dramatically the private sector's share of the education market. We find it deeply disturbing that public education, through charter provisions, might be contributing to the tendency to allow students to be taught in enclaves organized around narrow values or in environments from which many students may be excluded. Given the market-driven images for public education that seem to motivate many policy makers, it is time to ask, Is everything for sale in America—even access to decent schools and well-qualified teachers?[41]

Charter schools, like second marriages, represent the triumph of hope over experience. They have yet to prove they can deliver on their promise of a better education for those whom the public schools are failing. Yet there is strong public support for charter schools, and even though their worth is unproven, more charter schools open up each year than close down. Some observers see this as an ominous sign.

Charter schools are the death knell for public education because they siphon off human and financial resources and isolate communities at a time when the need for cohesion among public education's supporters is critical.[42]

Our hope is that the predictions regarding charter schools as the death knell of public education will be proved wrong—not because we yearn for the eventual vindication of charter schools but rather because we champion a victorious reinvention of the public school that will ultimately prove the charter school a costly and unnecessary experiment.

Schools for Profit

Into the face of hard truth flies the myth that if schools were only run in a more "businesslike" manner, the quality of education would improve. This myth is descended from the even greater myth that businesses, being profit-making organizations, run efficiently and inevitably produce superior products. Freed from the usual restraints of the public school, so goes the myth, privately run public schools could maximize efficiencies, increase accountability, and better focus on the needs of teachers, students, and parents.

Well, as bitter experience demonstrates, it doesn't often happen that way. A number of private companies have been formed—among them the Edison Project, Advantage Schools, SABIS Educational Systems, and Tesseract Group—all with the heady promise that they will deliver a new brand of educational success where traditional "bureaucrats" have failed. To date, despite the tens of millions of dollars invested, the for-profit school movement has been riddled with mismanagement, broken promises and, in some school districts, outright fraud. Between 1991 and 1995 the Edison Project alone spent more than $40 million before opening a single school. At the end of 1999, the company operated seventy-nine elementary and middle schools in sixteen states, with an enrollment of 38,000 children and contracted revenues of over $160 million,[43] yet its academic achievements have been few and far between. Advantage Schools, serving 9,000 students in eight states and the District of Columbia, has lost $30 million since 1997, and has fired its CEO. It is a company in trouble. According to an article in the *Boston Globe,* "Across the country, Advantage has made bold commitments, vowing to make stellar students of children victimized by the worst of public education. . . . But while promising to bring higher standards and sharper management of taxpayer dollars, Advantage has misled parents about teacher qualifications, failed to consistently boost scores on high-stakes tests, and engaged in financial practices that have prompted censure by at least two states."[44]

In even greater difficulty is Tesseract Group, formerly known as Education Alternatives, which is millions of dollars in debt, has laid off much of its staff, and has been booted off the NASDAQ stock exchange. It is still running schools, although it has filed for Chapter 11 bankruptcy. In the 1990s the company was promising to raise test scores in urban districts such as Baltimore and Hartford, and it won high-profile contracts there. After a disappointing performance, however, the company was kicked out of both cities. It headed south, to Arizona and Florida, where it concentrated on more affluent school districts. Yet even with tuition of $8,000 per student, money is so tight at the Phoenix area Ahwautukee campus, for example, that the school "can't afford the postage to mail report cards home." We don't have to worry about Tesseract's top executives, however. Despite the company's financial ills, founder John Golle made a net gain of roughly $1.75 million in 1993, thanks to having cashed in stock options when the share price was still relatively high.[45]

Operating in the U.S. through its office in Eden Prairie, Minnesota, SABIS Educational Systems manages schools in the United States, Africa, Europe, and Asia that educate 16,500 students worldwide. The United States is a relatively new market for SABIS, though it is running schools in Michigan, Massachusetts, and Minnesota and has plans to open charter schools in New York, Ohio, and North Carolina. Its track record is somewhat blemished because the largest approved charter school in Chicago terminated its contract following several complaints against the company and the state inspector general of Massachusetts released a report criticizing the company's questionable business practices.[46]

Some otherwise very smart people have woefully underestimated the enormous difficulties of creating and running a successful public school, and it would be sad enough if this were only a tale of political shenanigans and fiscal mismanagement. Horror stories lie behind the many failures of charter schools run by for-profit companies. Thousands of children and parents were lied to and then abandoned by school administrators to whom they entrusted their hopes for a better education.

We readily admit our strong bias against the very notion of public schools run for profit. The record shows that, in general, schools run by for-profit school management companies have not been shining examples of public-private partnerships. Yet fairness obliges us to point out that some charter schools run by for-profit companies, even those which are egregiously mismanaged, are a godsend to beleaguered parents, who consider almost anything better than the schools their children have been subjected to in the past. If this seems like a back-handed compliment, let the reader remember that were it not for the deplorable state of so many public schools, for-profit school management companies would have no reason to exist.

Incentives for Teacher Recruitment and Retention

The now widely recognized teacher shortage has caught state boards of education in a bind over recruitment versus retention. What to do first? Where should they spend the money? If you look at the shortage as a leaking pool with more pouring out the bottom than coming in at the top, then the problem is retention. If you're so desperately trying to get bodies into classrooms you have no time to think about strategies for plugging the leak, then the problem is recruitment. For policy makers, how to spend the money depends on where they stand and what choices they make. Mainly, educators and policy makers are talking about "getting the incentives right."

If you're on the recruitment side, you're thinking about how to get 'em into the tent. The one strategy that leaps immediately to mind is to raise teacher salaries. This is the option being tried in hundreds of school systems from Lincoln, Nebraska, where the minimum salary for a teacher with a bachelor's degree is about $21,000, to Yonkers, New York, where a first-year teacher with a bachelor's gets roughly $37,000.[47] Nationwide, the average salary for a beginning teacher with a bachelor of arts degree is $25,012.[48] At that level, though, how much can a salary be raised to make a real difference? The first-year teacher in New York City gets $30,100, whereas a few miles away in wealthy Westchester County, the new recruit can make up to $40,150.[49] How many of those teachers, given the choice, would rather teach in New York City?

Some districts offer signing bonuses to attract new teachers. The New York Board of Regents has recommended a $10,000 signing bonus for teachers who agree to work in high-need schools for three years. Several cities in Texas have offered signing bonuses of $1,500 to $2,000 to teachers who meet specific hiring needs, such as in secondary math and science. In Massachusetts, selected teachers new to the system are offered $20,000 to sign up; the bonus is meted out over four years.[50] This program has had some success in luring teachers to Massachusetts who might have taught elsewhere, but it has not kept unhappy teachers in the system once their stint is up, and the drop-out rate for novice teachers in their early years—even before they've collected their full bonus, is high. Twenty percent resign either during or immediately after their first year of teaching. Most often after receiving less than basic training (a six-week crash course held during the summer), they are ill prepared to handle the tough realities of classroom teaching.

Hayley Kaufman, a columnist for the *Boston Globe*, relates the experience of a friend of hers who, seeking a career change, was drawn to teaching by her high ideals and desire to "make a difference." She was among the 163 new recruits in Massachusetts in 2000–01 to accept the signing bonus, and she took a teaching job in a Cambridge middle school. After a horrendous first year, during which she received no mentoring and no support and met with a classroom empty of appropriate books and materials and administrative denial of extreme behavioral problems (don't call "unless there was blood on the floor," she was told), she's decided that no bonus can compensate for the life of a teacher in the public schools.

> She's walking away from the remaining $12,000 of her signing bonus and from her dashed hopes about making a difference—in a public school system, at least. Education Commissioner David Driscoll was quoted by the Associated Press as saying the only short-term answer to the state's teacher shortage is to "keep recruiting and offering bonus programs to draw people into the field." We can only hope that next they'll figure out how to keep them.[51]

Apart from signing bonuses, recruitment incentives can be varied and creative. Baltimore offers $5,000 in housing credits to teachers willing to work in hard-to-staff areas. New York, California, and other states have proposed tax credits and similar financial incentive packages to lure teachers, and a few districts have experimented with housing assistance and reimbursement for relocation expenses. The Los Angeles Unified School District helps teachers get home loans, find real estate agents, and generally figure out the home ownership process through the Los Angeles Teachers Mortgage Assistance Program. Some districts offer school loan forgiveness on a graduated scale in return for long-term contracts. Mississippi pays up to four years of tuition, room, board, and other expenses for undergraduate education majors at any public college or university in the state. Those funded for four years agree to teach for at least three years after graduation in an area with a critical shortage of teachers. In many districts around the country, bonuses are given to teachers who are NBPTS certified. Johnstown County, North Carolina, in addition to offering signing bonuses, has also compiled coupon booklets to welcome new hires, which feature, among other things, drugstore discounts and reduced-rate newspaper subscriptions.[52]

Responding to the opportunities presented by the teacher short-age, a multitude of independent agencies and consulting organizations have sprung up to help school districts and state departments of education recruit new teachers and assist with incentives packaging, brochures, direct mail, job banks, web sites, and other modern re-cruitment marketing tools new to the ed biz. For decades unaware of the impending crisis, education honchos have had to play catch-up in the hardball game of market competition.

All systems must recruit new teachers; those which can afford to take the longer view also think about teacher retention. Looking at the high drop-out rate for new teachers, a few states and districts are focusing on "induction" programs that are designed to orient, sup-port, assist, train, and assess new teachers in their first three years. An excellent idea, this approach is far from universal. Over half the states in the United States address induction in some way, but only seven states have both the mandate and the funding to support induction programs statewide. Ten states have a mandate but no funding, and another ten states have the funding but no mandate.[53]

Another strategy now recognized to be an effective tool in support-ing new teachers is mentoring—assistance, guidance, and nurturing provided by skilled professionals. The benefit of their experience can be invaluable, not only for the new kid on the block but for older teachers as well. Where there is good mentoring, the retention rate for beginning teachers is significantly improved, but mentoring, commonly practiced in other vocations and professions, is not wide-spread in teaching. Mentoring programs are included in the educa-tion agendas of about half the states; still, just having a mentoring program doesn't guarantee its effectiveness. Much mentoring is what professor Tom Ganser of the University of Wisconsin calls the Tom Sawyer approach.[54] Recall how Tom Sawyer got Huck Finn to help whitewash the picket fence? According to that method, a new teacher coming into a classroom is simply "handed a brush" by her mentor and encouraged to mimic what she does (thereby ensuring that bad habits and practices are handed down from one generation to the next). That half the states can stand up and say, "We've got mentoring!" doesn't mean much. Close examination reveals that most often mentors are given no training, supervision, or support; they are not paid or otherwise rewarded for their efforts; and no regular times are built into the school schedule for them to meet with those they mentor. In other words, even when mentoring is provided, it is seldom adequate.

Most incentives for teacher recruitment and retention are quick-fix solutions that qualify as Band-Aids.

Paying Teachers for Student Performance

Some "pay-for-performance" plans offer cash payments to teachers and administrators for success in boosting their students' scores on standardized tests. Advocates see such plans as motivational tools to increase teacher effectiveness. Not exactly a new idea, pay-for-performance was first tried in England around 1710.[55] Teachers' salaries were based on their students' scores on examinations in reading, writing, and arithmetic. This early system offering payments for results had great appeal because its goal was to keep children from poor families in school, where they could learn the basics. English teachers and administrators became obsessed with the system's financial rewards and punishments. Schools' curricula were narrowed to include only the basics, which were easily assessed and therefore more easily rewarded. Drawing, science, and singing disappeared. Teaching became more mechanical, as teachers found that drill and rote repetition produced the "best" results. In some cases teachers were led to falsify records by including names of good students who had died or who had moved from the district. Teachers deceived inspectors by signaling to children who were being examined when to multiply, add, subtract, or divide. This payments-for-results plan was ultimately dropped in the 1890s because it was judged to be unsound policy.

As if to prove the adage that no bad idea stays dead forever, the idea resurfaced in the United States in 1969 as "performance contracting." President Richard Nixon championed it, being concerned, as were the eighteenth-century English, over the lack of educational achievement among the growing population of urban poor. After a while it became apparent that financial incentives, while failing to produce the expected gains, were generating damaging educational practices, such as falsifying school records and teaching to the test to boost scores artificially. The inability of contractors to develop innovative teaching strategies and the dismal results doomed performance contracting. It was declared a failure.

> Why have so few schemes to pay teachers for their performance stuck? . . . Merit pay seldom works if its intent is to get teachers to excel, for little agreement exists among administrators and teachers about just what effective teaching is and how to measure it. In part, the complexity of the teaching act foils merit pay. Internal strife erupts over administrators' judgments when some teachers win "outstanding" marks and others only "average" grades.[56]

Nonetheless, pay for performance is a phoenix that continually amazes with its ability to arise from its own ashes. Frustrated with sinking school achievement, school districts around the country (Denver, Colorado; Fairfax County, Virginia; Hartford, Connecticut; and Montgomery County, Maryland—to name just a few) are currently enamored of this "new" idea—despite almost three hundred years of evidence that pay for performance has never positively affected the teaching and learning process. Even the Business Coalition for Education Reform, an alliance of thirteen national business-led organizations that strongly support pay for performance as a quality-improvement strategy, admits:

Pay for performance cannot address the whole range of teacher quality issues, nor can we expect it to solve the variety of teacher quality challenges our nation currently faces. A successful reform effort should also include a comprehensive plan to improve teacher preparation, provide ongoing professional development, and streamline teacher evaluation and removal procedures.[57]

Pay for performance erodes teachers' professional judgment and demeans education. It is just another counterproductive sideshow, a boondoggle that deflects us from reforming the education system at its core.

Teacher-Proof Curriculum

If teachers aren't teaching, and children aren't learning, then maybe we can fix the problem by handing teachers a self-guiding curriculum with as few opportunities as possible to screw up. So goes the theory of packaged curricula called sometimes curriculum in a box or, more often, teacher-proof curriculum, although that term is becoming outdated since its insult to teachers is pretty clear. The curricula in question are created by a growing and highly profitable industry dedicated to the development and distribution of the most effective teaching and learning tools money can buy. The intent is to turn teachers into vehicles for decisions made elsewhere and to help them march kids in lockstep from benchmark to benchmark, so that they will be ready for the next standardized test. These highly scripted programs contain no room for teachers' thinking or creativity or unexpected learnings that occur as part of a day in school.

After a decade of reform, we have finally learned in hindsight what should have been clear from the start: Most schools and teachers cannot produce the kind of learning demanded by the new reforms—not because they do not want to, but because they do not know how, and the systems in which they work do not support them in doing so. On the whole, the school reform movement has ignored the obvious: What teachers know and can do makes the crucial difference in what children learn.[58]

Proponents of these highly prescriptive programs where teachers must adhere to a strict, almost minute-by-minute set of directives for teaching believe that dollars are better spent on these curricula than on the needs of individual students. This kind of pedagogic uniformity interferes with the ability of a more knowledgeable teacher to work with children with different learning styles.

> There are several views of curriculum. . . . One is that teachers, especially elementary teachers, are so under-prepared . . . that the curriculum must do everything for them. It must tell them exactly what to do, when to do it, and in what order. Once this was called "teacher-proof" curriculum. Now, of course, that term is no longer fashionable, so teacher-proof-ness, when it is espoused at all, is couched in other terms. For example, a textbook representative recently described to me the lessons in their teacher's guide by saying, "And it's all scripted for the teacher, so that they know what questions to ask."[59]

Even as their effectiveness is being challenged, packaged programs for improving instruction and school management continue to grow in popularity. To a large degree, this trend is attributable to the now widespread use of standardized tests. Nationwide, students are failing these tests in appalling numbers and harried state boards are searching for ways to raise scores. That often means finding textbooks and materials coordinated with the tests, and then seeing to it that no matter what the weaknesses in instruction, students are going to acquire the information necessary to pass those exams.

In California, for example, the state school board rejected the recommendations of two review panels that gave high ratings to *Everyday Mathematics K–3*, a program deemed "exemplary" by the U.S. Department of Education. Over the strenuous objections of the California Mathematics Council, the board chose instead twelve textbooks, including two series by Saxon Publishers, a company specializing in skill building through repetitive practice, books that are considered "teacher-proof" because they include daily lessons and tests that eliminate the need for teachers to create their own. The state school board, it must be noted, is merely following the standards California adopted in 1998, which favor an instructional approach that reinforces basic skills and repeated practice of math functions rather than a conceptual understanding of mathematics and real-life problem-solving skills.[60]

Any intelligent educator should be suspicious of packages based on the presumption that a single method or approach could be best for every child in a district or school. That being said, however, we have looked closely and often quite critically at many so-called teacher-proof programs and have seen many of them in action. Too often, the only help the teacher gets is what's in her hands, and we have to ask ourselves if we wouldn't rather have a poorly trained, unmentored, and unsupported teacher with *something* to impart to her students than have her struggle with a curriculum she is unprepared to teach. At least the package is something that has been professionally prepared to compensate for insufficiencies in teacher training and expertise.

> It turns out that the single most important factor in student achievement is the expertise of the teacher. We used to think we could teacher-proof education, that we could somehow change the curriculum, change the textbooks, change the management system, and that would fix schools. And what we've learned in research over the last couple of decades is that in fact you can't improve education without investing in teachers who know a lot.[61]

Sad to say, until a significant improvement occurs in both teacher preparation and the practice of teaching, the use of "teacher-proof" curricula will continue to flourish under the guise of education "reform."

More Homework

It may appear odd to include homework under the umbrella of education reform, but the subject of homework has a hundred-year history in the United States and has always elicited strong feelings among those on both sides of the issue.

In an 1897 attack on homework, a doctor, Joseph Mayer Rice, wrote, "Is it not our duty to save the child from this grind?" In 1900 the U.S. Commissioner of Education testified before Congress that there should be no homework before high school. Between 1900 and 1915 *Ladies' Home Journal* took up the crusade against homework and enlisted both parents and doctors to back the contention that homework was damaging to children's health. Physicians declared that to be healthy, children need six hours of fresh air and sunshine a day. (Whatever happened to that idea?) At roughly the same time, a number of school districts around the country passed anti-homework regulations. In 1901, the state of California passed a law to abolish homework in grades K–8 and limit it in high school. During the 1920s, New York City banned homework in the public schools until the fourth grade. In 1930 the American Child Health Association classified homework as a form of child labor.[62]

Those anti-homework sentiments did not last long, however. By 1948 a national survey showed that the average amount of time that high school students spent on homework had risen to about three and a half hours per week. In 1957 the launch of Sputnik gave further impetus to the pro-homework movement by highlighting the concerns Americans had about keeping up with scientific advances, and the amount of homework given out by teachers jumped once again. By the time the 1960s arrived, the educational debate had shifted all the way from abolishing homework to reforming homework. In 1983, the national education assessment *A Nation At Risk* further spurred efforts to increase the amount of homework given in the nation's classrooms. By the 1990s a consensus seemed to have been reached, among educators and the public, that homework is in general "a good thing." A University of Michigan study found that although the amount of homework among high school students remained roughly the same between 1981 and 1997, the amount assigned to students aged six to nine had nearly tripled.[63] In 1994 the National Center for Educational Statistics reported that 46 percent of fourth graders spend an average of one hour or more on homework each day (37 percent spend half an hour or less, and 16 percent said they have no homework or do not do it anyway).[64]

In one century we have traveled from one view—that homework is bad—to its diametric opposite: homework is good. Several reasons account for this trajectory, given that the pressures for more and more homework come from all sides. It is the belief of many business leaders that the problems of poverty could be solved if students would work harder in school and at home and, as a result, reach the workplace better prepared. Teachers, under pressure from parents and administrators to "get more done," look on homework as a way to lengthen the school day and thus ensure that they can cover the full curriculum during the school year. Homework can also be seen as a way to involve parents in the education of their children—an effort sometimes viewed by parents as a technique for lazy or incompetent teachers to shift some of the burden of teaching onto their shoulders. Parents are not entirely blameless. Some who are ambitious for their children to get into better colleges by improving their grades and building better study habits believe that more, better, harder homework is the key.

Nevertheless, parental backlash against the ever-growing burden of homework is clearly spreading nationwide. "Help! Homework is wrecking my home life!" complains an article in *Education World*.[65] "Homework: time to turn it in"? asks the National Education Association.[66] The book *The End of Homework: How Homework Disrupts Families, Overburdens Children, and Limits Learning* was a bestseller.[67]

The school system causes many parents to feel shame and guilt because they haven't "made" their children do the homework. Schools and teachers tell parents that if they, the parents, had structured homework rules, the homework wars would come to an end. The assumption is that parents must be to blame for issues with homework. Parents are victims of a set of expectations that they cannot meet. Many parents feel homework is anti-family and they believe they are being held captive to the demands of their children's schools. Rather than being a time when families gather together, evenings have become battlegrounds in many households, as children and parents fight over getting the homework done. Tension and frustration run high. Parents feel they are being asked to enforce a practice whose value has not been proven, at least to them.

Current educational research tends to support their belief. What are the findings? That homework in the upper grades, in increasing amounts from the sixth grade through high school, is beneficial. In fact, it seems that the more homework, the better the chances of academic achievement. In the elementary grades, however, it's an entirely different story. Although there is evidence that *some* homework—twenty minutes a day or less—is beneficial, most homework assigned in kindergarten through fifth grade is an unwarranted, counterproductive, and sometimes harmful waste of time. The hour or more of daily homework assigned to nearly half the elementary students in the United States is an intolerable and educationally unwarranted burden on parents and children.

> My daughter was in kindergarten last year. . . . The philosophy of the program was that worksheets were not their ultimate goal. They felt that repetitious work should not take up time in the classroom, so the teacher sent that kind of work home. So every night my daughter had to do three or four worksheets . . . just practicing handwriting, copying letters, that kind of homework. I felt that for kindergarten it was a bit much. In the beginning there was a novelty factor, but then she began to say "I hate homework." It was hard to get her to do it.
> —Parent, Brooklyn, New York

Given the amount of attention paid to homework, and the increasing role it plays in the whole educational picture, it is surprising that the education of teachers does not include the subject of homework. Yes, that's right—except for a brief inclusion under the rubric of "classroom management," the whole subject of homework, including how to create and manage a program of effective homework, is not even addressed in college. What a teacher knows about homework she is likely to have learned from a single classroom teacher during her few weeks of practice teaching. As a result, teachers make up their own ideas about what homework is or should be. Given that teachers receive little or no supervision of any kind, they continue to do whatever they want, right or wrong, and to perpetuate whatever they believe to be appropriate, even though they have never been exposed to any systematic pedagogical approach to this whole area of education.

> My seven-year-old got an assignment to do a relief map of Massachusetts. First I, with her help, had to make the play dough . . . bake it for two hours. Terrific, an assignment that could only be done by a parent. I thought I had already gone to second grade. Then she was supposed to put in all the rivers and mountains by looking at a flat map. Imagine, translate a flat map to a relief map. Does any teacher think this kind of project is supposed to be done by a child? Or is the purpose for parents to pitch in and "do their share?" Am I supposed to be the teacher or a supportive parent?
> —Parent, Rockville, Maryland

School policies regarding homework are often inconsistent and weakly enforced. School districts articulate a homework policy but then do not follow through to see what actually takes place between teachers and students—and parents. Parents looking for consistency do not find it.

> With two girls in school I knew homework was going to be an issue when my oldest began the fourth grade, so I asked the teacher at the beginning of the year what the homework expectations were going to be

like. She told me she believed in giving about twenty minutes to half an hour of homework a night, and this seemed reasonable; however, it turned out to be incorrect. I don't know if this teacher is unaware of how long homework takes, or just says what she's supposed to, according to school policy, which I checked with the principal. All I know is, it takes the two of us fifteen minutes just to figure out how to do the assignment, most of which seems like a lot of busy work to me . . . endless "projects" like building a Greek theater out of sugar cubes or something. Homework for each of my children, the other is in the second grade, rarely takes less than an hour apiece and often longer. It just isn't right. Don't get me wrong. I think homework is important. But shouldn't it make sense?

—Parent, Rockville, Maryland

As if all the problems associated with homework weren't bad enough, homework also tends to widen the educational gap between the affluent and the poor. No matter how excessive the homework demands made by a teacher in an affluent school district, no matter how outrageous the waste of time or the requirements for materials, parents will dig deep to ensure that their kids don't fall short. As always, a so-called reform puts less advantaged children at a further disadvantage.

> Educational resources are distributed unevenly in this country. Some students go home to well-educated parents, access to tutors and computers with vast databases. Others have family responsibilities, parents who work at night and no educational resources in their homes. A principal once told us that he had solved the homework problem for poor kids—they just weren't assigned homework. This curious solution raises a troubling contradiction: either homework is of no educational value, in which case why is anyone doing it, or by not assigning it to the poor we are committing the worst form of educational discrimination by differentiating academic programs based on class. . . . Schoolwork should be done at school under the supervision of professional educators [and] where all students have equal access to educational resources.[68]

Homework, as it is currently assigned in the elementary grades, is both a boondoggle and a Band-Aid. Administered by poorly trained, unsupervised teachers, homework is too often excessive to a harmful degree, delivered by the incompetent to the unwilling, improperly meted out as a reward or punishment, based on educationally unsound principles, and used as a coverup for the shortfalls of inadequate classroom teaching. We agree with the authors of *The End of Homework*—"homework" should be carried out at school, under the supervision of professional educators. We would add one more thing. Those educators need to be supervised themselves, and trained to administer and correct homework, or the battle is only half won.

Homeschooling

Homeschooling is not a school reform but a rejection of public schools altogether. Nonetheless, because homeschooling is such a large and growing movement, no general discussion of education in this country would be complete without an examination of what homeschooling portends for the future of public schools. It is estimated that in 1980 the number of children being homeschooled in the United States was about 15,000. Today 1.2 million children, about 4 percent of the total K–12 population, are homeschooled. That's roughly the number of public school children in New Jersey—or, Alaska, Delaware, Hawaii, Montana, New Hampshire, North Dakota, Vermont, and Wyoming combined. Homeschool participation is growing an estimated 15 to 25 percent per year.[69]

What makes parents pull their kids out of public school—or not even enroll them in the first place? In a Department of Education study of homeschooling, a large number of parents said they teach their children at home for religious reasons. They want to provide their children with a curriculum oriented more toward their religious beliefs. Other parents say that they teach their children at home because they object to what is being taught in the public schools, or that public school isn't challenging enough, or that their child has special needs that aren't being addressed. Most strikingly, almost half of parents say they homeschool because they can give their children an education superior to the one they would get in their local public school.[70] They have little or no faith in the ability of public school to give their children a good education. Are they right? Can parents give their kids a better education?

Not long ago homeschooling was illegal in many states, and those who homeschooled their children risked censure and even jail. Today homeschooling is allowed in all fifty states, although the regulations regarding homeschooling vary widely. No doubt some homeschooled children are being shortchanged, but the overall report card on homeschooling seems to indicate that homeschooled children receive a better than average academic education. In 2000 MIT admitted seven out of twenty-one homeschooled applicants, and Harvard University has accepted students whose first experience in a classroom outside their own home is at college.[71] The Home School Legal Defense Association claims that on average homeschoolers outscore their public school peers by about thirty percent in all subjects.[72]

Evidence suggests that homeschooled children are socially "different" from kids who are subjected to the rough and tumble of social interaction in schools. Homeschoolers, however, respond that being herded together in same-age groupings is hardly a natural, real-life experience, and that the picture of a mother and her children sitting around a kitchen table does not do justice to the wide variety of learning opportunities homeschooled children can be given.

The greatest threat of homeschooling is not what it does to children but what we believe to be its impact on the health and vitality of the public schools. Funding for public schools is based on attendance, and the national average is more than $6,500 per student. That means homeschooling represents an economic loss to public schools of roughly $7 billion per year, not to mention the loss of a significant number of activist parents—those who are the most committed to their children's receiving a first-class education; those who, were they in the public schools, would be the front-line champions of school reform.[73]

Let us be clear on one thing: we do not advocate restricting, in any way, parents' First Amendment rights to determine through their own commitment of time, effort, and money, the course of their own children's education, no matter what form that might take. For a considerable number of families the public schools will never be the right choice. When one sets aside those whose deeply held religious, moral, social, or philosophical beliefs make the public schools anathema to them, however, an even greater number of families remain who would not resort to homeschooling if the public schools met their requirements for a quality education. These parents have abandoned the public schools because they feel that the public schools have abandoned their children.

It will not be easy to get them back.

Blaming the Unions

Teachers' unions have been demonized by their critics and canonized by their advocates. Anti-union folks, whether economists, social scientists, politicians, or members of the public at large, claim that the manipulative, power-hungry, bloated, tax-money-spending teachers' unions obstruct school reform and damage the quality of public education. From presidents to governors to mayors to superintendents to tub-thumping advocates of "school choice," union bashing is a popular sport. Here is Tom Ridge, as governor of Pennsylvania: "This is a debate about who controls the schools and who holds in their hands the destiny of our children. Does that control belong to the teachers' union or does it belong to parents, . . . to the taxpayers, . . . to school boards, . . . and to local business leaders who are working to improve public education?"[74]

The implication is not so subtle. If you aren't against the unions, you're against improving public education. Oddly absent from former Governor Ridge's equation are teachers, who apparently do not hold the destiny of Pennsylvania's children in their hands.

The argument is often made that teachers' seniority rights, conferred upon them by union contract, interfere with an administrator's ability to fire incompetent teachers. Bad teachers cannot be removed and good teachers advanced without a lengthy battle with the union. The dilemma is that according to long-standing labor laws, unions must represent teachers whose rights are violated, particularly if their jobs are threatened. Unions have a "duty of fair representation" and can be sued if they represent teachers in a perfunctory manner. Additional obstacles to removing teachers are state tenure laws, complex evaluation procedures, and principals' inability or lack of time to evaluate teaching effectively. To remove a teacher for incompetence requires mountains of paperwork and months of grievance meetings. Most principals (whose supervision is often cursory at best) simply are not up to it. To dismiss a teacher for "just cause," as unions insist, moral turpitude or criminal behavior must be proved; yet those are more easily provable than the intangible of poor teaching. Thus, it is true that unions act as a barrier to the removal of incompetent teachers. They also, it must be remembered, protect teachers against vindictive and arbitrary behavior on the part of supervisors who might want to fire teachers because of personality or philosophical differences—as well as reasons of race, religion, or sexual orientation.

Unions are also accused of purposely obstructing school reform by focusing on wages and job benefits instead of job performance. This charge has substance, for unions have been glacially slow, especially at the local level, to move beyond elemental trade unionism. Again, however, it must be acknowledged that teachers' unions became institutionalized because schools used to be horribly unhealthy places in which to work, and teachers were exploited and mistreated in the most degrading ways. And if anyone thinks those days are gone forever, sufficient evidence exists that where union protections are removed or waived (at charter schools, for example), school managements are not above overworking and otherwise exploiting teachers in the name of "the good of the children."

Is there a gap between the reality of teachers' unions and what people think about them? In a 1998 Gallup poll which asked Americans whether teachers' unions helped, hurt, or made no difference in the quality of U.S. public schools, 27 percent responded that unions helped, 26 percent that they hurt, and 37 percent that they made no difference (10 percent said they did not know).[75]

We find it fascinating that the public, if you take those opinions at face value, pretty much understands the impact of the unions on public education. In other words, in almost equal measure they help, they hinder, and they have no effect.

Teachers' unions are often thought of as a gigantic, monolithic enterprise with monopolistic power. In truth, there are two major national unions, the National Education Association, with 2.3 million members, and the American Federation of Teachers, with 940,000 members. Yes, they are large, representing 90 percent of the country's largest single occupational category.[76] With hundreds of local chapters, though, scattered around the country, each with its own autonomy and each subject to state laws, school district administrations, and local bargaining agreements, "the unions" are far from monolithic. Sometimes locals pay no attention to the national leadership whatever—to the chagrin of those at the top who claim to speak for their members. Members of union locals have a mind of their own, as was dramatically demonstrated in 1998 when the leaders of the NEA and AFT decided that a merger of the two unions would be beneficial for both and, after a full year of intricate negotiations, put it to their members for what they thought would be a rubber-stamp vote. In an unprecedented rejection of a leadership-backed initiative, the rank and file turned the merger down.

Teachers and their unions have a long and complicated history.

The first collective teacher organization, which eventually became the National Education Association, was founded in Chicago in 1857. More of a professional association than a rank-and-file trade union, it was directed mostly by white male college presidents and school superintendents until the beginning of the twentieth century. The American Federation of Teachers, established in 1916, had roots deep in trade unionism. Led by more-radical female elementary school teachers, the AFT joined forces early with the American Federation of Labor and fought successfully for improved working conditions and decent living wages for teachers.

After woman suffrage and the ratification of the nineteenth Amendment in 1920, the two unions fell into a relatively passive phase until the 1960s, when states began passing legislation that permitted collective bargaining by teachers' unions. Modeled on the 1935 National Labor Relations Act, this form of collective bargaining, *industrial bargaining,* emphasized the exclusive domains of labor and management with their ritualized pattern of demands, rebuffs, and concessions. With industrial bargaining, teachers won the right to organize and negotiate over wages, hours, and working conditions. Teachers gained a fairer and more reasonable work environment, but their contracts also limited the scope of their work—not only what they were required to do but also what they were *allowed* to do. In the long run, a system that functioned for factories or the factory model of schools is now widely understood to cause dysfunction in today's schools. Industrial bargaining remained prevalent in all school districts until the 1980s and persists in many districts today.

Since the mid-1980s there has been an effort by union leaders to transform teachers' unions from their industrial-era ideological base to organize the work around quality teaching. Unions, at least at the national level, came to understand that standards had to be raised if public education was to succeed. Simultaneously, there has been an attempt to regard teachers as professionals and individuals, as knowledge workers rather than industrial workers. Both labor and management now make deliberate and collaborative efforts to empower teachers and engage them in the school reform movement. It was the expectation that the scope of this *reform bargaining,* as it has come to be known, would expand beyond the conventional bounds of wages, hours, and working conditions and strive to improve the quality of teaching and learning in schools.

Industrial unionism and industrial management assume a division of labor in which school districts prepackage the curriculum and where teachers, like assembly line workers, implement that curriculum. The "new unionism" assumes a more professional stance in which educational decisions are made in the classroom by teachers rather than decided centrally and dictated downward.

Both the NEA and the AFT are calling for union members to rally behind the cause of higher standards for teachers. As early as 1985, AFT president Al Shanker supported tests for new teachers because he foresaw the day where standards would be lowered in response to the teacher shortage "unless a new and better exam is created."[77] Shanker was also an early advocate of using the power of unionism as an engine for reforming education.

The two unions understand that establishing high standards is not the hard part of education reform. The hard part is bringing more than the top 15 percent of students to a higher level of academic achievement. That can only happen if union issues are organized to focus on teacher quality. Standards need to be backed by adequate training, professional development, and a strong peer review system. In each of those areas, the unions are now devising strategies, developing programs, and actively participating in the process in line with their own best interests. Results are spotty but encouraging.

The AFT set up a task force to study and monitor the issue of teacher preparation, and among its recommendations is a ten-point program that would include toughening the academic standards in teacher preparation and encouraging closer cooperation between colleges and schools to create a more rigorous clinical experience for new teachers. The task force calls on the union locals to assume greater responsibility for working with districts and colleges to identify and train higher-quality teacher candidates.[78]

In support of professional development, the AFT has set up Educational Research and Development programs that (the union claims) provide professional development training and resources for teachers in a hundred school districts.[79]

Also at the district level, some union locals are coming around, albeit slowly, to support the notion of peer review. Peer review requires teachers themselves to make decisions about what constitutes good teaching and makes provisions for teachers with expertise in their subject area to evaluate and assist weaker teachers. Although peer review appears in only a few district contracts, it is potentially the most powerful innovation that the unions have made since collective bargaining and the institution of tenure. Ultimately, it requires teachers to make decisions about removing (or counseling or training) colleagues who cannot perform. This radical departure from established industrial norms more nearly resembles the way guild unions function. The purpose of peer review is to raise the level and protect a standard of teaching.

The AFT affiliate in Toledo, Ohio, pioneered peer review in 1981 by creating the Toledo Plan, in which consulting teachers assist and evaluate new teachers as well as veteran teachers. New teachers also have the option of continuing to meet with their mentor during their second year of teaching. The Toledo Plan is now one of the best-known peer-review programs in the country and has been praised by the National Commission on Teaching & America's Future.[80] In both Toledo and Columbus, Ohio, the union claims that peer review has brought higher standards to teaching. In fact, more probationary and experienced teachers have been dismissed under peer review than under the previous system of administrative review. In addition, these programs are effective in retaining teachers, both novices, who experienced a better induction as a consequence, and experienced teachers, who are given a variety of responsibilities. According to John Grossman, president of the Columbus Education Association (the NEA local), "PAR [Peer Assistance Review] has clearly stabilized the teaching force. When we started, the average experience of teachers in Columbus was six or seven years. Now it's well over fifteen. We've gotten people off to a strong start."[81]

In several other instances, union initiatives help dispel the myth of unions as self-serving organizations that militate against reform. Both the NEA and the AFT, together with school districts, are working collaboratively on improving low-performing schools. In 1999, for example, New York City schools negotiated an agreement with the United Federation of Teachers that gave the union a substantial role in transforming low-performing schools. According to the agreement, the district and the union would jointly develop a plan for improving fifty-one low-performing schools. The district had wanted to "reconstitute" those schools by removing faculty and staff and hiring a new group of teachers and administrators. Under the agreement, class size in the schools was reduced and schools implemented research-based mathematics and reading programs. The two sides agreed to lengthen the school day to provide for additional instruction time and professional development. The district agreed to provide some incentives, including higher pay to encourage teachers to apply to teach at the low-performing schools. In the first year the fifty-one schools in the program improved their performance at a rate twice that of comparable schools. The improvement slowed in the second year, but the schools continued to improve. According to Heather Lewis of the Center for Collaborative Education, United Federation of Teachers union president Sandra Feldman set the tone for the collaborative venture. "She used the union presidency as a bully pulpit. She went public about the data, the number of failures, the dropout rate. She was not defensive, not protective of bad practice or poor student outcomes."[82]

Pay for performance is a school reform initiative that unions historically characterize as merely a form of merit pay which would rely on subjective evaluations of teachers. Nonetheless, the union in Denver, Colorado, negotiated a contract that included pay for performance (teachers would be paid differentially, and effectiveness would be rewarded). If the majority of a teacher's students improved over the course of a year, the teacher would receive an additional $1,000. The Cincinnati Federation of Teachers, working along with the district, developed a system of "pay based on knowledge and skills and group bonuses linked to school performance," which it adopted in 2000.[83] The plan was resisted by many within the district, however, and the union president was defeated for re-election as a result. This does not bode well, even though district officials are confident that pay for performance will remain in the contract. As we have already stated, we do not think that pay for performance is a good idea. We mention this saga, though, as evidence that unions can, when pushed, exhibit flexibility in their response to calls for school reform initiatives.

In some districts unions have supported the notion of "within-district charter schools." In an effort to maintain innovation in public schools without moving to school privatization or charter schools, the Boston Teachers Union, working collaboratively with the Boston School Department, established pilot schools—that is, public schools with more liberal contracts. Freed from many school department and union regulations, these schools are designed to foster innovation. Initially, six pilot schools were negotiated as part of the contract; the number is now eleven. Though standardized test scores have not yet improved in these schools, all of them are popular alternatives to the regular public schools and have waiting lists of students.

Both the NEA and the AFT have endorsed certification standards promulgated by NBPTS and support legislation to encourage teachers to become certified. Some districts have bargained for salary incentives based on demonstrated high-quality practice in exchange for board certification. In this way administrators can offer teachers additional salary for increased expertise without opening up the Pandora's box of merit pay. In addition, through their role in the National Council for Accreditation of Teacher Education, the unions are working to set high standards for who can become a teacher. The argument against such union activism is that creating higher standards will result in even greater teacher shortages along with pressure for higher salaries. That may be true, but we challenge anyone who sees a danger that teachers might be paid too much to stand up and say so with a straight face.

Organizing around educational quality has been a challenge for the few districts in which unions have risked this dramatic shift in philosophical approach. Unions cannot set aside the traditional (and still important) issues of work, rules, and salary but now must add educational quality to the complex mix. Despite reform efforts included by both the NEA and the AFT in their national platforms, local unions today, like the schools, more nearly resemble those of yesterday than ever before. The failure of most locals is that they still expend most of their energy and resources on defending a very small minority of troubled members: most locals still narrowly define their mission around bread-and-butter issues and often confine themselves to reacting to management's actions and provocation rather than taking a more proactive role. Schools in this country are a maze of rules and hierarchies, and unions take their form and function from the school districts within which they exist. Neither schools nor unions can change without the other's changing because of the industrial mind-set in the United States and our industrial-era labor laws.

Yet despite substantial changes in the attitudes of national union leaders and the willingness of a few local unions to try new approaches, when unions finish describing the long list of reforms they have implemented, the cold hard fact remains that little has changed in the vast majority of American schools.

Unions are neither all good nor all bad, and those who oppose them or support them are neither all right nor all wrong. Still, when one is shooting from the hip, it is easy to aim for the largest target.

Teachers' unions are a convenient scapegoat for frustration over the ills of public education. But they are not the cause. As John F. Kennedy said, "Mythology distracts us everywhere. For the great enemy of truth is very often not the lie: deliberate, contrived, and dishonest. But the myth: persistent, persuasive, and unrealistic."[84]

It will be no easier for unions to change their culture than it will be for the public schools to change theirs, but precisely that kind of change will be required if both are to survive and prosper in the new millennium.

Here is our cue to introduce the Millennium School.

6 The Millennium School: A Total Approach to Solving the Fundamental Problems of Elementary Education

The wise learn from the experience of others, and the creative know how to make a crumb of experience go a long way.—Eric Hoffer

---

When America was an agrarian society in the throes of building a new industrial age, the goal of its education system was to keep as many children in school as possible. Over the past 150 years that goal shifted. Now the goal is academic success for all children; however, the nature of schools and schooling has not changed to accommodate this more recent philosophy. That is why placing more and more demands on a system that is unable to respond adequately will continue to have a deleterious effect on student (and teacher) achievement. Improved student learning will take place only when teachers have access to the necessary training, knowledge, skills, working conditions, and material resources. For them to have the tools they need, major changes must be made.

A New Model for a New Era

We propose a model of public education that calls for reinventing the elementary school, and doing it all at once. Let's do away with the

Band-Aids and boondoggles, the costly and poorly considered reforms that go nowhere, and put the brakes on the continuing cycle of failure—the Trilemma Dysfunction. History has shown rather conclusively that, when only one reform is attempted, that reform is ultimately diluted and then defeated. The reason all currently proposed education reforms are ultimately doomed to failure—the reason they will not solve the deeply embedded problems of today's schools—is that they are all modern accessories grafted onto an obsolete model that is fundamentally unsound. Public education is a Model T Ford—an excellent machine in its time, but woefully inadequate for the needs of contemporary society. In an attempt to improve its performance, we've implanted an automatic transmission, installed halogen headlights, air-conditioning, disc brakes, radial tires, and the latest high-tech shock absorbers, even thrown in computerization. But we've ended up with a hybrid that costs more, runs no better, still causes constant frustration to its owner, and consistently underperforms. If we are to reach our destination—a consistently dependable system of quality education for all American children—then we need a different machine to get us there. We call this new model a Millennium School.

In a Nutshell

- A Millennium School offers teachers a multilevel career path that rewards advanced training and experience with higher levels of pay, responsibility, supervision, and team management.
- Teams are composed of teachers and interns at different levels, along with specialists to deliver coordinated programs and curricula to students, provide supervision and mentoring to associate teachers and interns, support the principal with progress and achievement reports, and integrate accountability into teaching practice.
- Teachers receive meaningful professional development through

such vehicles as alternative professional time and grand rounds, which provide opportunities for teachers to do research, peer coaching, and curriculum development.

- A Millennium School is structured to be small, in order to be responsive to the needs of teachers, students, and parents. It serves as a locus for community services and optimizes the school year to incorporate time for extra student and teacher learning.

- Millennium Schools reverse the current trend in which under-qualified teachers enter the classroom. They help professional-ize the practice of teaching and draw better-qualified candi-dates into teaching by providing visible and clearly defined career opportunities.

What will it take to create a Millennium School?

First, Give Teachers a Real Career

The primary requirement for turning teaching into a career is to offer a highly visible and clearly defined career path, with opportunities, rewards, and advancement for teachers *who continue to work in the classroom, teaching children.*

A career with a clear trajectory offers the opportunity for increased responsibility, salary, and status commensurate with increased skills and demonstrated performance. It also helps ensure greater account-ability for all teachers. In a Millennium School, supervisory teaching positions allow teachers to share the responsibility of evaluation with the principal who, when working alone, never has the time to pro-vide meaningful assessments of teacher performance.

A Millennium School calls for the establishment of six teaching positions:

Chief instructor
Professional teacher
Teacher
Associate teacher

Teaching intern
Instructional aide

Each position has its own job description, stipulated level of professional training and achievement, and licensing requirements. A Millennium School thus eliminates the typically "flat" organizational structure prevalent in almost all schools, regardless of size, in which the principal directly supervises all teachers. Can you imagine a business organization, even a small one, that depends on the CEO's supervising each employee, or even every department manager? The CEO would be so overwhelmed that she would not be able to accomplish other important tasks. Delegation is essential. In large schools, the principal may be responsible for supervising sixty to eighty teachers, specialists, aides, substitutes, and other personnel. This makes no sense. In a Millennium School, the principal directly supervises only the chief instructors, who are responsible for the performance of their teams.

Chief instructor. A chief instructor (C.I.) is a team leader, supervising a team consisting of professional teachers, teachers, associate teachers, and interns. The chief instructor's license, based on certification by NBPTS, is gained only after five years' experience as a professional teacher, plus intensive study, and represents the highest grade in pay and the highest level of achievement in the teaching profession. A chief instructor must be expert in the areas of content, curriculum development, student learning, and assessment and must demonstrate the ability to translate relevant and accepted research into practice. The chief instructor must also provide tangible evidence of contributions to the profession, including research, publications, university teaching, and presentations at conferences. Working an eleven-month year, the chief instructor has as primary responsibilities supervision and mentoring—assisting colleagues, giving demonstration lessons, observing, coaching, and facilitating curriculum and staff development.

Professional teacher. A veteran teacher with a master's degree and several years' experience, the professional teacher (P.T.) is certified by NBPTS and is licensed as a supervisor for intern teachers and a mentor for associate teachers. The professional teacher has developed and continues to maintain a teaching portfolio that tracks professional progress; has passed a competency exam in all subject areas; and has passed a rigorous performance assessment either at the school or at a regional testing center. Responsibilities include classroom teaching, with one or more of the following options: supervising interns, mentoring associate teachers, and engaging in teacher research or curriculum development, or both.

Teacher. A license to attain the level of teacher requires a minimum of two years' teaching experience, a master's degree, and performance assessments that include a work portfolio of videotaped lessons, written evaluations, and student work. A teacher may remain at this career level or prepare to become a professional teacher. Some teachers would rather spend their professional lives providing direct service to children exclusively through classroom teaching; the position of teacher gives them that opportunity. The teacher need not seek advancement to the higher level of professional teacher. For many teachers, the rigorous requirements of attaining NBPTS certification and the added responsibilities of mentoring and supervising required of a professional teacher are simply not a career goal.

Associate teacher. In today's school structure no distinction is made between the raw novice and the veteran. Every teacher, at every level of experience and expertise, has the same responsibilities. The position of associate teacher acknowledges that a new teacher needs a period of time in which to become "encultured," supported by supervision and instruction from an experienced mentor—a role filled by both chief instructors and professional teachers. In a Millennium School, associate teachers (A.T.'s), although fully accredited, carry less than a full teaching load. Time not spent teaching is spent observing other teachers in classroom settings, attending workshops and seminars, and engaging in other forms of professional development. After an intense two-year period of extended learning for the beginning professional, the associate teacher assumes the role of teacher and may elect to begin the process of becoming a professional teacher.

Associate teachers can enter teaching by one of two pathways: the traditional route, through a university graduate or undergraduate teacher education program, or some alternate route. They may be recent college graduates (of the Teach for America program, for example), candidates seeking a midcareer change, or retired professionals from other backgrounds who are interested in a teaching career but would find it onerous to undertake a full university program at their stage in life. Many states have aggressive programs to recruit such candidates, but, poorly prepared, they rarely get the support they need on the job, while they are still learning to teach. A comprehensive approach supports both traditional and alternative entrants to the field and creates an expanded pool of high-quality teachers. In a Millennium School, associate teachers are integral members of a teaching team and pair up with professional teachers to co-plan and team-teach lessons. A chief instructor provides a minimum of five hours of demonstration lessons per week in the associate's classroom.

An associate teacher's license requires a bachelor's degree and demonstrated teaching proficiency. Those taking the alternate route to teaching must have a provisional teaching certificate, which they acquire through six course-work credits plus six weeks of classroom teaching experience during the summer before they start work.

Teaching intern. Interns are either graduate or undergraduate students who work full-time for at least a year in the classroom as part of a degree program at a nearby university. Teaching interns are not accredited.

For those who follow the traditional route to teaching, through the college, the "clinical" aspect of teacher training (hands-on classroom experience) and the academic component of teacher education made possible through the school-college collaboration are important prerequisites for successful teacher training. Just as brain surgeons cannot master the skills they need merely by attending lectures and reading textbooks, teachers need to gain classroom teaching experience by spending the bulk of their time in a "real" school as functional members of a teaching team. They are not on the fringe of school life but are considered to be junior faculty with responsibilities for the instruction of children. These include classroom teaching part-time, under the close supervision of a professional teacher.

Instructional aide. The instructional aide assumes a number of support tasks during the school day, such as leading a variety of small groups and providing curricular support to children, under the close direction of the teaching team. She teaches reading and math groups, supervises children during lunch and recess, and provides clerical assistance to the entire team.

Substitutes. In theory, through the benefits of team teaching, a Millennium School could eliminate substitute teachers and the headaches and costs attendant on the substitute system; however, we know that in the real world this expectation would be highly unrealistic. If substitutes were eliminated, then, when teachers were absent, A.T.'s or interns would have to take up the slack in the schedule. Such a misuse of their valuable time would undermine their important learning process. Substitutes may still be necessary, depending on the size of the school and the composition of the teaching team, but it should be possible to reduce reliance on substitutes significantly.

Second, Make Teaching a Real Profession

In order to improve public education, indeed to ensure its very future, we need to professionalize the practice of teaching. But isn't teaching already a profession, you might reasonably ask? No, unhappily for everyone, it is not. In one sense, of course, teachers are "professionals" in that they get paid for what they do, as opposed to amateurs, who do not. That distinction, however, is better applied to endeavors such as astronomy and golf. Is teaching comparable to such "true" professions as medicine and law? Jon Saphier, an articulate and tireless advocate for the professionalization of teaching for over twenty years, points out that a profession:

- Has a recognized knowledge base
- Demands rigorous training and certification of its members
- Fosters a culture of consultation and collaboration in the workplace
- Systematically indoctrinates and "encultures" new members
- Requires that continuous, regular learning be built into the work cycle
- Has high public accountability, and takes full responsibility for outcomes
- Internally maintains high standards of practice
- Has members who make autonomous decisions guided by an agreed-upon canon of ethics[1]

None of these characteristics can be claimed for teaching. How, then, can the practice of teaching be so thoroughly overhauled that it will fulfill every one of these criteria and thereby transform teaching into a profession?

Acknowledge that teaching is a complex skill that requires specialized training. Once we understand that teaching is much more than simply conveying information from one person to another, certain truths begin to emerge, and persistent myths disappear. One myth is that anyone can teach, as long as he or she is reasonably bright and knows the subject matter. In truth, not everyone is cut out to be a teacher. Just having gotten all A's in science or math does not automatically make someone a good candidate for teaching science or math. Pedagogy, the art and skill of teaching, requires its own knowledge and training, separate from those pertaining to the subject being taught. Because the quality of teacher education is frequently so appallingly poor, a current of opinion among some of the public, and among too many policy makers as well, holds that we should recruit teachers from among the brightest of the population who have had no teacher training and should bypass education schools as a source of future teachers. This is a short-sighted, self-defeating, and wrong-headed approach, which overlooks the fact that teaching is a skill that must be learned in order to be practiced successfully. ("Hey, I was the successful CEO of a Fortune 500 company. Now let me perform brain surgery!")

Teachers in training should earn a bachelor's degree in an academic subject, followed by a master's degree in education to qualify for certification. Standards for admission to graduate schools of education should be made considerably tougher than they are today, and the standards for licensing teacher training institutions also must be raised.

Improve teacher training through professional development schools. It makes no sense that the colleges charged with educating classroom teachers are so distant from the practical process of teacher preparation, or that novice teachers, fresh from graduation, are thrown into the classroom to fly solo with so little in-class training. That is why professional development schools (school-college collaboratives) are the key to improving teacher education.

When schools and colleges collaborate in placing teaching interns in working classrooms, making them full participants in team-teaching environments where they receive expert mentoring and supervision while practice-teaching, several benefits are attained.

The most immediate benefits accrue to the classroom teachers and students. Teachers receive extra assistance and support; students receive more individual attention, more stimulation, and a greater variety of educational experience. Benefits to the school include the automatic increase in school staff, a consequent reduction in substitutes, and the increase in scheduling flexibility. The benefits that have the most far reaching effects, however, are those which occur over the long term. Professional development schools raise the level of the profession by putting more practiced and skillful teachers into the field. They establish an educational continuum that begins with teacher preparation and continues with ongoing professional development for experienced teachers. Professional development schools participate in building the professional knowledge base that is crucial to the cultivation of teaching as a profession.

Employ team teaching. Numerous studies conducted both in the United States and in other countries, notably China and Japan, have shown that teachers become more proficient by continually working on curriculum, demonstration lessons, and assessments together.[2] Research shows that not only does working in teams improve the practice of teaching; it also eliminates the isolation inherent in most teachers' work lives.[3]

A Millennium School relies on a team-teaching structure, with each team consisting of one chief instructor, four professional teachers (one of whom is a special education teacher, one a professional teacher with arts expertise), one teacher or associate teacher, and two teaching interns. Three teams share a full-time media specialist. Each team serves approximately 120 students. The team is a group of teachers organized to work together in a multifaceted enterprise, with joint responsibility and public accountability for results with children. Much as hospitals are now being held accountable for patients' recovery rates, the teams will be held accountable for students' learning.

For the teachers, team-teaching means meeting as a group to grapple collectively with concerns and questions and arrive at solutions. It means writing new curricula collaboratively, implementing established curricula in new ways, planning and teaching lessons together, conferring with the special education teacher, taking responsibility for the progress of special education students, and supervising full-time student interns.

The Millennium School team-teaching model helps teachers establish strong relationships with each other and gain expertise through ongoing professional dialogue. Team teaching allows teachers to achieve new levels of professional communication and accountability. Children learn more by being exposed to an expanded range of teaching styles and broaden their social experiences by working with students from different grade levels and classes. And the close interaction that takes place among teachers, interns, and college faculty improves teaching methods and skills.

Institute peer coaching and grand rounds. Peer coaching is a process through which two or more colleagues work together to share pedagogical knowledge and increase their technical repertoire. In plain language, that means formalizing a way in which people who work in the same building can get together as colleagues to help each other out. In peer coaching, the focus is on the teacher as a learner. Teachers reflect on current practices, build new teaching skills, improve instructional strategies, and match teaching strategies to individual differences among children. Peer coaching provides teachers with opportunities to try out new ideas or different approaches and discuss the results with a colleague.

Teachers are forever going to workshops, but endemic to the practice of teaching is the difficulty of converting workshop knowledge to classrooom practice. Peer coaching helps individual teachers successfully import their training into their classrooms. Peer coaching creates an environment in which school people can collaborate as "critical friends" who examine in a nonjudgmental fashion one another's practice and help improve it. Peer coaching allows teachers to share successful practices in a forum for addressing instructional problems. The goal of peer coaching, in addition to improving the practice of teaching, is ending the school culture in which every teacher must struggle alone through the early years of practice with a frustrating trial-and-error method of learning.

Peer coaching does not just "happen," of course; it is scheduled and supervised by the chief instructor, who is in turn responsible to the principal for accomplishing peer coaching initiatives.

Like peer coaching, grand rounds help to end the culture of isolation by making teaching a more public act.[4] Based on the idea of rounds made by physicians and interns in a teaching hospital, grand rounds are regularly scheduled classroom visitations by teaching interns, associate teachers, and professional teachers, sometimes joined by visiting educators. A professional development innovation of a Millennium School is that, during grand rounds, teachers teach individual lessons while other teachers observe. The group subsequently examines and analyzes the lesson. Through grand rounds, more experienced practitioners can pass on knowledge and experience to the less experienced. Grand rounds encourages teachers to observe, discuss, and analyze teaching, a process that in turn allows them to create strategies to improve their own teaching.

Provide alternative professional time. Alternative professional time (APT) supplements teachers' classroom work with additional responsibilities—something that many teachers desire—and allows teachers to learn new skills and gain experience in areas of special interest, such as teacher research, curriculum development, and mentoring.[5] Teaching interns, who assume some teaching duties by mid-October of a school year, help make the time available.

No teacher is required to take alternative professional time, but APT does provide opportunities for those who want to enrich their professional practice with new educational experiences, make connections to the broader worlds of research and practice, or conduct research and publish their work.

Integrate meaningful professional development into every teacher's work life. In most states, physicians are required to take a certain number of hours of continuing medical education each year to maintain their certification. In theory, teachers get recertified in much the same way—by taking courses relevant to their practice. In reality, however, the rules are so relaxed that teachers are often allowed to take courses that have nothing to do with education or teaching. Moreover, when education is the subject of teachers' study, their professional development does not build on what they already know. Rather, the emphasis is on correcting presumed errors, "fixing" what the teacher is doing wrong. Every year there is a new technique, a new "fix." Teachers watch fads come and go; most are Band-Aids that rarely improve practice in the long run. Professional development is not development at all, but merely remedial instruction. As a result, teachers stagnate.

A Millennium School incorporates professional development into the daily schedule of the workplace, by combining such innovations as grand rounds and peer coaching with more traditional after-school and summer workshops to give teachers numerous opportunities to improve their teaching practice. Another vehicle for learning, the case study, enables teachers to analyze the strengths and needs of children who are experiencing difficulties in their classrooms and to seek assistance from other members of their team in solving the problems. In addition, district or regional professional development labs provide opportunities for teachers to practice their craft in a setting outside the school.

High-quality professional development motivates teachers to improve their practice by identifying what they need to know and do to promote student achievement and by providing the necessary tools and resources for professional enrichment.

Incorporate teacher research. In the education world, educational research is conducted "from above"—that is, by experts who may or may not ever have been classroom teachers themselves and whose findings are published in journals rarely read by teachers.[6]

A Millennium School creates and nurtures conditions under which research by teachers can flourish. Research is an integral part of the school's norms, and not just another fad that will disappear in a few years.

Educational research (conducted by teachers during APT time) validates the voices of teachers and raises the level of professional development from remedial to professional. Teacher research starts where the action is, and recognizes that the practitioner's wisdom is a valid source of knowledge about teaching.

When teachers conduct research into their own practice, their role expands: they become more than "deliverers of knowledge." They create knowledge by working on research in their classrooms and across schools and communities. They assume responsibility for systematic research and inquiry directed at the improvement of their practice. Teacher research creates a model for problem identification, problem solving, and theory building, by using research data to improve student learning rather than relying on decision making based on "seat-of-the-pants" reckoning.

Supervise teachers and hold them accountable to standards of performance. The organizational structure of a Millennium School supports open accountability. Implementation of the middle-management position of chief instructor ensures meaningful, ongoing supervision and thus holds teachers accountable. Where teaching is a public act, no teacher can hide behind closed doors, and that openness helps create and maintain a culture of accountability. Principals and chief instructors identify weak teachers through consistently maintained documentation and then offer guidance and assistance so that they can improve their practice. Working as members of a teaching team and teaching in classes observed by colleagues, as opposed to teaching alone behind closed doors, force teachers to sharpen their teaching skills and maintain a higher level of performance.

The National Board for Professional Teaching Standards has established a definitive set of teaching standards, along with testing methods for measuring a teacher's ability to achieve them.[7] Unfortunately, in many states the standards and the test are well-kept secrets. In a Millennium School, however, every teacher must be board certified to attain the status of professional teacher. The certification and recertification of teachers is rigorous and performance-based, ensuring that teachers keep abreast of current educational ideas and teaching strategies and that they know their subjects and how to teach those subjects to students.

Measure student progress. In a Millennium School, there is a peer review of every child's progress. That is, more than one person is responsible for a child's learning. Progress is measured through standardized test data, together with class performance indicators. *Both the school (principal and middle management) and its teachers are held accountable for a year's educational growth for each child.* If that growth does not occur, the causes must be determined and a remediation plan developed. Teaching strategies are reviewed; children's work is analyzed; families are brought into school. Children must be at grade level before they are promoted. Children who do not achieve a year's growth must participate in remedial programs, including summer school and after-school tutoring. Accountability eliminates the practice of "social promotion" and assures that every child reaches her or his potential. In a Millennium School, no child slips through the cracks.

Third, Improve Educational Leadership and School Management

Give the principal a new job description. Reshaping the job of the principal, along with reshaping the job of the teacher, can bring better candidates into the profession and vastly improve American education in the new century. In the Millennium School, teachers work and think in entirely new ways, so the principal's job needs to change as well. The Millennium School principal is a team player and an educational leader, not an autocratic, top-down decision maker.

First, to reshape the job of principal, teaching and training must allow candidates to learn how to be a different kind of executive. A principal's training must create a new kind of supervision that models how to share power, how to work as a member of a team, how to collaborate with chief instructors and teachers of other ranks in the new workplace with differentiated staffing, and how to increase leadership capacity among teachers.

Second, the new model for the job of principal will include regular peer coaching and mentoring of principals as part of their professional development. The role of the principal must be "recultured" to build networks of principals, so that they can enjoy the same kind of problem-solving assistance and support that their teachers are receiving in the new school culture.

Third, the facility manager (see next section), relieves the principal of the responsibility for building operations and maintenance that acts as a drain on time and energy and diverts attention away from the vital task of providing educational value to the school. This shift in responsibilities gives the principal time to fulfill the job's central role to strengthen both the collective learning of the staff as a whole and the competence and commitment of individual staff members. The principal, along with the teaching faculty, collaboratively develops and supports the vision for the school. The principal consistently emphasizes a clear intellectual mission and, together with the instructional chiefs, hires staff to teach toward that mission.

As the Millennium School's educational leader, the principal knows what is going on in each classroom and is the ultimate authority on accountability. The principal meets weekly with the chief instructors to discuss supervisory and curricular issues. He or she works on a sustained basis with the weakest teachers to improve their teaching. The principal also acts as mentor to chief instructors and others who may want to change their career objectives and become principals themselves. The principal is also the primary liaison with the community, informing parents of school goals and addressing parents' concerns.

Eliminate the vice-principal and add a facility manager. There is no vice-principal at a Millennium School. That onerous position is no longer required. Too often the vice-principal has been set up as the "enforcer," whose main responsibility is discipline and coercion, but who also tracks maintenance problems. What the overburdened principal needs more than a vice-principal is a facility manager.

A study of the job of the principal revealed that 58 percent of a principal's time is devoted to management responsibilities.[8] As we have noted, the principal is too often sidetracked into solving urgent problems of facilities management. The specially trained facility manager assumes most of those responsibilities, so that the principal can devote more time to matters of education. The facility manager supervises the custodian and internal maintenance people. He or she also deals with the city public works department about such issues as snow plowing and maintenance of sidewalks, driveways, parking lots, and playgrounds. The facility manager also administers contacts with such vendors and outside service people as carpenters and electricians and the heating specialists who maintain the physical building and grounds.

Make the most of space and time by restructuring the school into smaller schools. Education in America has been shaped by the energies and philosophies of the industrial age. Chief among these was the creation of the egg-crate school in which the ideology of mass production was applied to the configuration of individual classrooms separated by age groups, without regard for whether the practice was educationally sound. A persistent refrain of American business since the beginning of the twentieth century has been "the best product at the lowest price." Somehow, however, in translating the business credo for educational practice, "best product" was left out, and only "at the lowest price" was retained. One victim of this credo has been the small school. Since World War II, a period of rapid population growth, the *number* of schools in the United States declined by 70 percent, while average *size* increased 500 percent. Since 1945, the number of school districts has been consolidated from more than 100,000 to just 15,173 in 1992.[9]

There is no educationally defensible reason for maintaining elementary schools of a thousand, two thousand, or three thousand students; as a matter of fact, such schools are organizationally, educationally, and culturally unsound. We understand why they continue to be built—the cost and difficulty of acquiring real estate, the economies of scale involved in building one or two large buildings instead of several smaller buildings and hiring nominally smaller staffs (fewer principals and custodians), and the educational establishment's cultural predilection for centralization of power and control. But just because big schools are expedient does not make them good. In the long run, it does not make them more economical, either.

Research conducted over the past thirty years has shown that students in small schools (four hundred to six hundred students) earn higher grades, come to class more often, participate in more extracurricular activities, and are less likely to drop out than those who attend larger schools. Teachers are more satisfied with their jobs at small schools and collaborate with one another more. When cost is measured per graduate rather than per attendee, small schools are more efficient than large schools.[10] As educator Deborah Meier notes, "In schools, big doesn't work, no matter how one slices the data. Large schools neither nourish the spirit nor educate the mind. . . . What big schools do is remind most of us that we don't count for a lot."[11]

A small school is a facilitating condition for a strong professional community. Students can't get lost in a small school, and they can't hide. The small school supports teacher accountability. Responsibility for students' learning at small schools is collective and more collaborative. Teachers and parents alike know who teaches well and who does not, which teachers are prepared, which ones are inspiring and effective, and who goes the extra mile for a child. Both teachers and parents are given an opportunity to participate in a process that takes corrective action where needed. In a small school, all students are known. Small schools offer physical safety to children because everyone knows who belongs in the school and who does not. Parents have easy access to teachers and the principal, and school staff members know all the parents. Parents can get to know their schools through direct observation, not only through homework, teachers' reports, and test scores. In addition, the marketplace provides the positive aspects of competition necessary to make small schools work harder and smarter.

We also maintain that for small schools to operate even more efficiently (offer the best product at the best price), they must be given sufficient autonomy; each school must have responsibility for budget, staffing, scheduling, curriculum, and assessment.

We do not advocate emptying all the big schools in the United States and building smaller schools in their stead (although doing so would reduce the danger, expense, and annoyance of busing). It is not necessary to build new buildings in order to create smaller schools. Existing large buildings can be divided into smaller entities—two schools sharing the same building, for example—and models for this type of schools-within-a-school configuration already exist in many parts of the country.[12] Small schools are not necessarily more expensive than larger ones and their creation does not automatically increase the school budget.

Provide a better community services facility. The American elementary school was designed for a society that no longer exists. Schools are empty a significant part of the week and year, while outside their walls social needs are poorly coordinated and unmet. Schools are particularly underutilized as providers of child-centered services to families.

The idea of making better use of public schools as "community schools" offering a comprehensive set of family support services is not a new one in education circles, but a Millennium School is especially well suited to this model. With its culture of teamwork and shared goals and ideals, the school is a locus for child advocacy. Assuming an advocacy role means making sure that certain services are provided—not necessarily that the school itself provides the services, but that the services are offered within the school community, with the school at its center. A Millennium School is a primary resource in providing physical and mental health-care support services to the whole family. Special programs, including English as a second language and literacy classes for families, a lending library, and intergenerational programs, are an integral part of the full-service school that includes before-school and after-school programs, social services, day care, preschool, extended-day and extended-year schooling, elder services, and adult education.

The better the school and its attendant social and educational activities are integrated into the community, the better are family-school relationships, and the more successful is the learning of the students who attend. In most communities, school buildings are among the most significant capital expenditures. Until they are better utilized, they will continue to provide a less than optimal return on investment.

Extend the length of the school day. Primarily for economic reasons, the length of the school day has remained constant, while demands on the time available during which the teaching must take place have enormously increased. The school day is constantly interrupted for "pull-out" kids who need instruction in English as a second language or special education or computer training or counseling. We fervently believe in the philosophy of "mainstreaming." That is, kids should not be pulled out of class for special instruction. Yet because those are critical needs that must be met, how and where are those services to be provided? The answer is, partly by specialists working in conjunction with the teachers, in the classroom, and partly supplemented by after-school programs where they do not interfere with classroom activities and academic subjects. Scheduling in a Millennium School seeks to protect the school day (8:00 A.M. to 3:00 P.M.) from incursions into teaching time by lengthening the time the building is open and scheduling all nonclassroom activities, functions, and programs after 3:00 P.M.

Table 6.1. The Millennium School Day

Time Period	Activity
7:00 A.M. to 8:00 A.M.	Meetings
	Parent conferences
8:00 A.M. to 3:00 P.M.	Regularly scheduled classes
3:00 P.M. to 6:00 P.M.	Homework center
	Remediation: special education, English as a second language
	Social work and counseling
	After-school care
	Clubs
	Extracurricular activities and sports
	Parent conferences
6:00 P.M. to 10:00 P.M.	Adult education
	Community outreach
	Parent conferences

In addition, to accommodate the school's role as the focus of a child-centered community facility, the school building must be open from 7:00 A.M. until 10:00 P.M. Table 6.1 sets out the schedule of a typical Millennium School day. The period from 7:00 A.M. to 8:00 A.M. is flextime, reserved for team meetings, meetings between the principal and the chief instructors, lesson planning, professional development, before-school tutoring, and parent conferences. Classes are held from 8:00 A.M. to 3:00 P.M. The period 3:00 P.M. to 6:00 P.M. is reserved for a broad range of after-school activities. Homework, the source of tension and discord in so many families, is fully supported at an on-site homework center. Children are not pulled out of class for remedial work; those services are delivered before or after school. Certified teachers are available during these times because their schedules are staggered, some teachers starting work later than others. Sports, clubs, music, art, drama, and other activities flourish in the extended portion of the school day. Lengthening the school day accomplishes two major goals; it brings schools and school systems into realistic alignment with the rest of society, including businesses, which have changed to accommodate the needs of working families, and it increases remedial and enrichment opportunities for students and teachers.

Reconfigure the school year. A Millennium School follows the traditional September-to-June school year, but summer programs are added. Summer school, for example, is mandatory for students who are not achieving grade-level reading or mathematics at the end of their school year. The objective is to eliminate "social promotions" by ensuring that kids actually do acquire the academic skills they need to pass into the next grade.

Summer school for teachers is also an option. Summer curriculum workshops and professional development opportunities are provided for all teachers who wish to take advantage of them. If they want to upgrade their professional status (from associate teacher to teacher or from professional teacher to chief instructor), this is where they spend the time.

A Day in the Life of a Typical Millennium School

To demonstrate how a Millennium School would function in real life, we created the Mary McCloud Bethune School, filled it with six hundred students, staffed it with faculty, made it a professional development school in collaboration with Chicago University (our invention), and set it in motion. This is how it works.

At 6:15 A.M., as Gloria Amparano pulls out of her driveway on her way to work, her mind is on the day's schedule. Principal of Mary McCloud Bethune School, a K–5 professional development elementary school in a diverse and densely populated suburb of Chicago, she is one of the most experienced and best trained of the principals to head a school based on the Millennium School model.

This is Monday, so her first meeting is from 7:00 to 7:45 with her

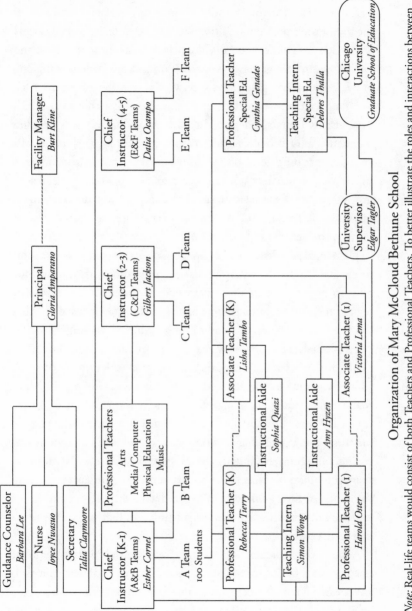

Organization of Mary McCloud Bethune School

Note: Real-life teams would consist of both Teachers and Professional Teachers. To better illustrate the roles and interactions between the *new* job categories, this chart shows no Teachers on the A Team.

staff of chief instructors, a cadre of three career teachers who are at the top of their profession in training and experience. Esther Cornel is the C.I. for grades K–1, as Gilbert Jackson is for grades 2–3, and Dalia Ocampo for grades 4–5. Each team is cross-graded, consisting of two classes at one grade level and two classes at the other level. One teaching team is assigned to each grade level, so chief instructors supervise two teams. They are directly responsible to Dr. Amparano for their teams' progress. Each team comprises professional teachers—the next rung down on the professional teaching career ladder—in addition to teachers, associate teachers, instructional aides, teaching interns, and special education teachers. Music, art, computer, physical education, and media teachers, who are shared among teams, provide services to the team.

Dr. Amparano (let's call her Gloria, as does everyone in her school) thinks back to her first years as a principal and how hard it was not only to get started, in those days before principals had access to regular mentoring, but also how hard it was to stay focused on what she felt was her primary responsibility—educational leadership. So many obstacles stood in the way: one crisis or another always derailed her efforts to set academic goals and measure achievement. She was so overwhelmed by the demands on her time—scheduling, building maintenance, cafeteria management, and a thousand other operational and noneducational issues—that she never had the time necessary for planning, teacher supervision, and building a community of teachers and learners. Teacher supervision? It was a joke. No business manager would be expected to supervise, review, and assess the performance of fifty to sixty employees. Yet in the flat organizational structure of schools when she was starting out, that was what principals were expected to do.

When the concept of distributive leadership came along, championed by educators such as Richard Elmore at Harvard, she welcomed it. It ran counter to the way she had been trained as a principal, yet she had always believed that leadership, as

Elmore put it, constituted the guidance and direction of instructional improvement. Distributive leadership depends on multiple sources of guidance and direction, made coherent through a common culture.

In taking on the principalship at Bethune, Gloria had accepted a whole new way of thinking. She worked in collaboration with teams in a less hierarchical school structure, which negated the idea that power is a zero-sum game—that is, that there is only so much of it to go around. In fact, when power is shared, the degree of leadership *expands*. The more leaders there are, the more leadership is available. The new Millennium School model that Gloria has learned to work so well with is a fine example. She no longer feels the burden of directly supervising fifty teachers, interns, student teachers, aides, special education teachers, art and music instructors, and custodial staff. Doing so is no longer her job alone. Rather, supervisory duties are distributed among mid-level managers, such as chief instructors. The chief instructors supervise the professional teachers, who supervise the teachers and associate teachers, who participate in supervising interns and instructional aides. Like good middle managers, the chief instructors are responsible for the performance of their teams, but they too share power, leadership, and responsibility.

At a traditional school, when a child fails, who is responsible? More telling, who is *accountable?* In a Millennium School, *everyone* is accountable. A client is served by a team of attorneys and other legal professionals. A patient is served by a team of doctors and other medical professionals. At Mary McCloud Bethune School, a student is served by a team of teachers and other education professionals. At a traditional school any teacher, working mostly alone and virtually unsupervised, can pass along any unsuccessful learner into the next grade. Hardly anyone notices. If anyone does, well, it was not her fault! It was the fault of the teacher before her—and before him, and before that. At Mary McCloud Bethune School, the failings of any child do not go unnoticed. No one falls through the cracks. Academic achievement, or lack of it, is tracked by more than one person on each team, and everyone on the team is accountable for each child's success or failure. Team members work together to resolve the issues that stand in the way of every student's progress.

At 6:50 Gloria pulls into her parking space and walks up the stairs toward her office. As she passes the facility manager's office, she pokes her head into the cramped but neatly organized space to say hello to Burt Kline. Although they often solve emergencies and small problems on the fly, Gloria and Burt also meet regularly, every Wednesday at 4:00 P.M. to review the current state of the physical plant and discuss actions taken on matters already identified. With the creation of the facility manager's position (which they can well afford, because the school has no vice-principal), Gloria no longer bears the burden of managing any aspect of maintenance and repair, which now fall squarely on Burt's shoulders.

Walking past the school secretary's desk, Gloria grabs the sheaf of pink messages and blue to-do notes from Talia's outstretched hand as she strides into her office. At 7:02, her staff of chief instructors is waiting for her.

Gloria has spent the past several years taking courses, upgrading her skills, and studying the literature on educational leadership and school reform. Richard Elmore's treatises are among her favorites, and she has memorized a whole list of what she has come to call Elmore-isms. One of her favorites is "Isolation is the enemy of improvement." The team-teaching approach implemented at Bethune, in which chief instructors manage teams of teachers, has broken the barriers of isolation to allow the creation of a school culture that looks on improvement as a goal not only for students but for teachers as well. Curiously, in most discussions about school reform, the definition of teacher *improvement* is rarely discussed, except in reference to curriculum. The notion that education is about real improvement is hardly entertained.

In most schools, if a student finishes first grade with a C average, the expectation is that if the next teacher can manage to keep the child at the same level before passing him into third grade, then she's done her job. Conferring with the first grade teacher (or anyone else) to find out what strategies might bring the student up a level in academic achievement is not even on her radar. Improvement isn't a goal. At the same time, teacher improvement is also not an expectation. In most schools there are no institutionalized mechanisms for improving a teacher's practice, because *improvement* is not considered to be an activity in which a teacher must constantly be engaged.

These thoughts run through Gloria's mind as the meeting gets under way. The main topic of this morning's meeting is progress and intervention strategies for associate teachers. This is an analysis and review of each team's associate teachers, given by each C.I. after having consulted with the A.T.'s supervising professional teacher, and by observing the A.T.'s work in the classroom. Chief instructors meet with their two teams' professional teachers every Friday morning from 7:00 to 7:45 to review the progress A.T.'s are making toward their individualized goals. What specific skills is each working on? What strategies are the P.T.'s employing to help strengthen them in their weak areas? Do any problem areas need immediate attention? How can they support the P.T.'s? They gather the information they'll need to make their reports at the Monday morning staff meeting with Gloria. During the week, chief instructors will meet individually with each of their professional teachers to work on their ongoing professional development.

Associate teachers are beginning classroom teachers who are potentially on a track to become professional teachers, the level at which most teachers will probably want to remain for the rest of their professional lives. At some point in their careers they will decide whether or not they want to work toward becoming chief instructors. Doing so will require not only considerable time and effort but a significant change in their responsibilities.

Newly hatched college graduates, clutching a degree in one hand

and a teaching certificate in the other, enter the Bethune School with the understanding that for the first few years of their career they are still in the beginning stages, in the process of acquiring professional skills. They will teach a class four and a half days a week, and their chief instructor will teach their class for half a day. On that half day, the A.T. will observe either her own class being taught by her C.I., or possibly, another class being taught by another C.I.

Esther Cornel, C.I. for the two K–1 teams, talks first about her A.T., Lisha Tambo, who has clearly increased her repertoire of class management strategies, thanks to the ongoing support of her P.T., Rebecca Tierry, an excellent mentor. Rebecca has given classroom demonstrations of cooperative learning, had Lisha try them with the class, and then given Lisha feedback. Rebecca is proud of Lisha's success, for it reflects well on her mentoring skills, and the better Lisha gets at teaching, the stronger the team becomes. At times Lisha handles the classroom alone, and the students come to understand that they are being served by two teachers instead of just one. Rebecca reports that Lisha has organized cooperative learning groups and that they are running smoothly.

The other A.T. on Esther's A Team is not faring so well, because her professional teacher is dealing with an especially difficult class and has had less energy to mentor his A.T. Harold Oster is a good mentor, but the challenges of his class have interrupted the flow of communication between him and his A.T., Victoria. Victoria's strength is math, and her writing instruction is not strong. Esther reports that she's instituted regular Tuesday afternoon meetings with Harold and Victoria and is also conducting demonstration lessons on writing instruction for both Harold and Victoria to critique, thereby giving Harold some relief from his mentoring responsibilities without taking over the job of supervising Victoria. Esther reviews her strategy, which includes modeling a mini-lesson, allowing for independent work, providing critical feedback and peer conferencing, and summarizing the lesson. Esther finishes her report with a review of the A.T.'s on her B Team, and the other C.I.'s, Gil and Dalia, deliver their reports as well. Both Esther and Dalia ask Gloria to conduct demonstration classes for their A.T.'s some time the following week, and they agree on a schedule.

As the meeting moves on to other topics, Gloria reflects on the difference this school model has made in the lives of the teachers and the impact it has had on their professional practice. In most schools, Lisha would not have been an associate teacher but a struggling first-year teacher with little if any direct supervision. Gloria knows that she would have been inside Lisha's classroom a few times a year, for maybe thirty minutes each time. If Lisha were lucky, she and Gloria might have had one or two meetings, and she would have received a written evaluation based on little more than a minimal understanding of her skills and her worth as a teacher. The principal would have become aware only over time of her reputation among parents, and possibly through other members of the teaching staff. Lacking mentoring, support, or critical feedback, Lisha would either have repeated her mistakes year after year, tried out different approaches on a hit-or-miss basis, in hopes of succeeding, or gotten frustrated and burned-out and, like 50 percent of all new teachers, quit within the first five years. If she were really smart and talented and self-motivated, she might even have evolved into an excellent teacher on her own. As we have seen from our examination of teaching elsewhere in this book, though, there is little reward for self-motivation in the prevalent school culture.

In the case of the associate teacher, Victoria, who is good at teaching math but needs help with writing instruction, most schools would have no mechanism to provide the support and assistance critical to Victoria's improvement. At Bethune, her P.T. and C.I. both supervise her work, give her feedback, and provide demonstration lessons. The expectation is that Victoria will improve her teaching, and that it is the job of the senior members of her team to help her by providing *multiple sources of guidance and direction.*

While Gloria meets with her chief instructors, other meetings are taking place throughout the building. Not all meetings are rigidly scheduled, but team members are required to meet—both formally and informally—on a regular basis. Professional teachers, associate teachers, teaching interns, instructional aides, and specialists are meeting to plan lessons, give feedback and instruction, evaluate parent conferences, and collaborate on solving problems of classroom management.

Teachers working in teams and using meetings to plan classes, implement curriculum, identify problems, and share solutions are not the norm in public schools. At Bethune, teamwork is embedded in the organizational structure and in the culture. In most schools, for example, art teachers work in a different part of the building, and their programs in no way intersect with the curriculum of the classroom teacher; nor do art teachers and grade-level classroom teachers work out strategies to integrate their teaching. Bethune School provides both the time and the encouragement for collaborative work. It is also rare, in most schools, for special education teachers to meet regularly and work closely with classroom teachers in coordinating their efforts to modify instructional methods and materials for the special students in whom they share a common interest. At Bethune, specialists are members of the teaching team, not remote providers of services outside the purview of classroom practice.

The implications for teaching and learning are enormous. Connections are made—between math and social studies, between music and history, between art and social studies, between science and language arts—that are possible only when contributions from various sources are coordinated and comprehensive. The net gain accrues to both the teachers and the taught.

The meeting adjourns shortly before 7:45, and Gloria checks her schedule against the tidy stack of to-do notes and messages on her desk. She has to squeeze one hour of preparation time into her day because tomorrow she is teaching her once-a-week course in American History to the two fourth grades of Dalia Ocampo's F Team. Another Elmore-ism comes to mind: "Where learning is the shared responsibility of the leaders, then the leaders are required to model the learning they expect others to engage in." In Gloria's school, everyone teaches. The chief instructors teach one day a week. Nurse Joyce Nwasuo teaches a third grade class in health and nutrition, and facility manager Burt Kline teaches a unit on electricity as part of the fifth grade science curriculum. Even Barbara Lee, the school social worker, works with groups of students on social interactions and school-community issues. From top to bottom and from side to side, Mary McCloud Bethune School is a community of teaching and learning.

As they leave their Monday morning meeting with Gloria, the chief instructors head in different directions.

This morning C.I. Esther Cornel is observing Simon Wong, a teaching intern, as he teaches Harold Oster's first grade class. It is close to the middle of the school year, and Simon is now ready to handle a class on his own, with minimal support. Harold is not teaching his class today because he is working on his alternative professional time (APT) research project. Harold is conducting a study on the self-perception factors underlying motivation and achievement among African-American elementary school students (are you just "born smart" or can you "get smart?"). Professional teachers have six hours a week of APT time on school time to work on their professional development, during which time they are exempted from their classroom teaching responsibilities. It gives interns the opportunity to teach a class solo, and to have a C.I. observe them and provide feedback. One of the benefits of becoming a professional teacher is having APT time, which assumes a level of professionalism not yet achieved by associate teachers. (Yes, *APT time* is a redundancy, but after wrangling with it, the teachers just gave up.)

Gil Jackson, C.I. for the second and third grade teams, is teaching a demonstration class in math for his third grade associate teacher, who has been having difficulties with the new math curriculum. They have discussed math instruction strategies in a previous planning meeting, and Gil is going to demonstrate for the A.T. how to implement them. Coincidentally, this is a particularly good time for Gil and his A.T. to be concentrating their attention on math, because math is the focus subject of this month's grand rounds. Once a month the principal and the chief instructors decide what the "theme" of the following month's grand rounds will be. When the focus subject of the grand rounds is announced, each team is responsible for coming up with its plan for grand rounds. That means simply that teachers plan to make four of their classes in math available for observation during that month, and they post the dates and times on a central board, along with a brief description of what they will be teaching. Every professional teacher, associate teacher, and teaching intern is required to visit three math classes during the month.

Grand rounds serves several purposes. Perhaps most important, it institutionalizes and perpetuates the norm of teaching as a public act. It also gives teachers a set of opportunities to observe and learn from other teachers, to reflect on their own practice, and to become further encultured in a community where they all participate in the twin acts of teaching and learning. This is an extended community because Chicago University, Bethune School's partner in the school-university collaborative that manages graduate school teacher education, also participates in grand rounds. Several times during the year, Edgar Tagler, a professor at Chicago University and supervisor for the collaborative's teaching interns, visits a grand-rounds lesson with an intern. This morning, in fact, C.I. Dalia Ocampo is meeting with Ed Tagler to review, among other things, scheduling for Ed and her teaching interns during the upcoming grand rounds. There are twelve interns at Bethune, and Ed represents their connection to the academic institution from which they are being weaned as they make the transition to the real world of classroom teaching.

Using professional development school standards as a guide, Ed maintains weekly contact with each of the interns, observes their teaching a minimum of six times a semester, confers with them in three-way meetings with their supervising P.T.'s, and grades their work in collaboration with the P.T.'s, as well. Far from being viewed as an outsider who makes occasional incursions onto grade school turf, Ed Tagler is a constant presence at Bethune School. Not only does he interact with Bethune teachers on a regular basis; he is also a valuable resource for teaching expertise. Ed's special academic interest is in science, and when the school has a science grand rounds, he teaches a demonstration lesson for the interns and other teachers.

One measure of how well this professional development school relationship between school and university is working is the changed attitudes of the teaching interns. Formerly, student teachers (as they used to be called) felt no allegiance to the elementary schools in which they taught while they were fulfilling the student-teaching component of their education. The classrooms they visited—one can hardly say they "taught" in them—were merely way stations on the path toward obtaining a degree. They thought of themselves as college students, not contributing members of a teaching team. Now their allegiance is twofold. Yes, they are students at Chicago University, but Bethune School is "their school" and, as in the Beach Boys' song, they're true to their school.

Chicago University has no trouble recruiting candidates for the school-university collaborative program offered by the university's graduate school of education. Although teaching interns receive paid tuition credits for their teaching work at Bethune, the main attractions are the opportunities to participate in a particularly rigorous program with high standards of achievement (placement is highly competitive) and to teach as a member of a team where interns are treated as professionals; Bethune's reputation is also key: graduates of the Bethune program are highly sought after for teaching positions throughout the country. The intense full-year internship at Bethune not only puts these apprentice teachers far ahead of graduates from other programs in terms of classroom teaching experience, but also offers exposure to innovative approaches to teacher education, enhanced learning situations for teachers and students, and a broad range of teaching styles.

In Gloria Amperano's mind, one of the most interesting organizational improvements at Bethune, and one she stresses to the candidates she interviews for teaching positions, is the practice of "looping." Looping keeps a class and teacher together for two school years, so that a teacher on the K–1 team, for example, teaches kindergarten the first year, then keeps the same class for her first grade the following year. When that year is finished, the teacher moves back to kindergarten and takes a new class, passing her class on to the team for grades 2–3 and starting a new "loop." It is the teacher, in fact, who does the looping. The class keeps moving ahead. Looping has several benefits. First, the practice builds closer bonds among students, teachers, and families. Besides, it saves valuable time. In every two-year period, at least a full month is saved the second year because the teacher already knows everyone's name, personality, social skills, learning style, family situation, and level of academic achievement. That is like adding three full months of good teaching to every student's K–5 schooling experience. Looping also increases teacher accountability. No longer can any teacher blame a child's weaknesses and failures on what the previous teacher didn't teach. Perhaps most important, when both teachers and children are able to form a longer-lasting relationship, teaching and learning opportunities are both broadened and deepened. Table 6.2 provides a summary of the benefits of a Millennium School.

How Much Will It Cost?

The casual reader will look at all the new positions created at a Millennium School and gasp. Where will we get all the money for

Table 6.2. Problem and Solution Summary: The Benefits of a Millennium School

Current Problem	Millennium School Solution
Egalitarianism The pervasive cultural norm of equal status prevents teachers in their everyday interaction from discussing their work or collaborating on shared problems. Observing some teachers do something new or different and getting attention and respect for it intensifies others' turf protection and feelings of powerlessness. Teachers don't learn from one another; every teacher invents her own practice from scratch.	*Recognition for Career Achievement* Roles are differentiated on the basis of clearly articulated standards and certification. Teachers' individual areas of expertise are recognized and valued. Experienced teachers counsel novice teachers, regularly observe one another teach, and give one another feedback. Teachers gain increased responsibilities and rewards consonant with increased skills and capabilities.
Isolation In the segmented structure of the "egg-crate" school, with its secretive compartments, each role is isolated and competitive.	*Teamwork and Collaboration* Conditions of work support continuous professional growth and organizational effectiveness. The workplace is intellectually challenging; teachers work in teams to make teaching more "public"; teachers venture beyond the classroom. Shared responsibilities and widespread interaction among teachers strengthen teachers' influence on one another and on the school.
Poor Teacher Preparation Colleges of education graduate poorly trained new teachers who, increasingly, come from lower and lower ranks in their class. Band-Aid solutions to teacher education programs are ineffective.	*More Rigorous Training* The quality of teaching improves as colleges of education engage with classroom teachers in discussions about teaching and improvements in instruction and curriculum. As student scores rise, parents demand

Table 6.2. Continued

Current Problem	Millennium School Solution
	schools where teaching matches the high-quality collaboration and results of the Millennium School. In a classic example of "market pull-through," teacher preparation programs are forced to do a better job as the demands for quality that are placed on them increase.
Little or No Mentoring New teachers sink or swim. The belief is that the novice teacher with a license is fully qualified to teach without further assistance or support. Alone in their classrooms without support, many novice teachers give up before they have acquired the skills necessary to teach. As the teacher shortage increases, new teachers are hired in greater numbers, less qualified than their predecessors, and then leave in ever greater numbers. To compound the problem, little is done to identify the skills of potential mentors, adequately train mentors, or provide time for them to do their jobs.	*Mentoring as an Expectation and the Norm* Novice teachers, who do not at first teach full-time, have the support of a well-trained mentor: a professional teacher. Beginning teachers have ongoing opportunities to continue their learning, so that they can become more skilled more quickly. The professional teacher, responsible for mentoring, has achieved NBPTS certification, has been trained in mentoring new teachers, and has the time during the school day to work with them. The professional teacher is not only a role model and an advocate for the associate teacher, but an evaluator as well. Thanks to the team structure, all planning is done collaboratively, so the novice teacher is mentored both by other members of the team and by the professional teacher.
Weak Professional Development In most school districts, professional development is designed to be "one	*Professional Development as Integral to the Career* Professional development is focused

Table 6.2. Continued

Current Problem	Millennium School Solution
size fits all" and is characterized by "one-shot" workshops and the "flavor-of-the-month" trend in education. Professional development is treated as an add-on program rather than as part of the daily job of the teacher. Teachers have no follow-up help during the implementation phase and little continuity in building their practice. Professional development programs have minimal impact on teaching quality.	on deepening knowledge of subject matter and improving teaching skills. It is a continuous process, collaboratively determined by teachers expert in their academic areas, knowledgeable about the school district's curricular and instructional needs, and up-to-date on current educational research. Professional development is embedded in day-to-day activities: teachers hold curriculum conferences to develop teaching materials and assessments and look at student work. Professional development is further enhanced through research that teachers conduct on their daily practice.
No Career Ladder Teaching is a flat career and therefore not attractive to the academically able student. The job on the first day is the same as on the day of retirement. Increased skills do not bring additional responsibilities.	*A Clearly Defined Career Path* A career ladder provides increasing responsibilities as teachers move up the rungs from teacher to professional teacher to chief instructor. Along the way, individuals at higher levels provide support. The professional teacher mentors the associate; the chief instructor mentors the professional teacher. Improvement of skills is recognized and rewarded. For those who want a Peace Corps style of experience for a few years, the associate teacher role is perfect. Candidates receive intensive instruction before starting to teach; there is regular supervision and training

Table 6.2. Continued

Current Problem	Millennium School Solution
	once the novice is on the job—the associate teacher is surrounded by the guidance and support of veterans.
	For those who see teaching as a life-long career, clear steps are set out; guidelines and assessments assist teachers along the way; and licenses—professional teacher's license, mentoring license, chief instructor's license—mark the stages of achievement.
Lack of Accountability When students don't learn, schools blame the family, society, the student, the previous teacher. Schools should be held accountable for the learning of children, but aren't.	*Everyone Accountable* Where teaching is no longer a private act, the accountability is higher. In the Millennium School, teachers are regularly observed by their colleagues as well as by their supervisors. Appropriate responses to weak performance range from additional mentoring and training to termination. Students' progress is carefully monitored in many ways, from standardized test scores to performance-based assessments.
Incompetent Teachers Not Removed Inadequate supervision and union tenure laws allow weak teachers to continue teaching without either support or repercussion.	*Incompetence Not Accepted or Tolerated* With greater time and expertise applied toward supporting and evaluating teachers, everyone is expected to improve. Those who don't are counseled to leave teaching. Historically,

Table 6.2. Continued

Current Problem	Millennium School Solution
	principals have had limited time and expertise to assess teaching performance. The new role of chief instructor helps fill that gap. An effective, nonbureaucratic system exists for removing incompetent teachers. Unions are involved in the process, and their role in blocking dismissals is minimized.
Teachers at the Bottom of the Power Structure Teachers make decisions only about classroom policy; what to teach, how to use time, and how to assess progress. All other decisions that affect teachers' work—scheduling, class placement, assignment of specialists, professional development, and the allocation of budgets and materials—are made at higher levels of the school bureaucracy. The norm by which teachers are powerless to affect schoolwide policy is widely accepted by teachers and administrators. This view of power as a zero-sum game in which a gain in one area requires a loss in another causes conflict between principals and teachers. When principals fear they will be relegated to becoming professional managers as teachers assume new leadership roles, they vigorously oppose such changes.	*Decision-Making a Shared Responsibility* Through the team structure, all teachers have voices in decision making. Assisted by a cadre of chief instructors, and a facility manager to take care of operations, principals are able to take their rightful place as instructional leaders.

these new job categories? is likely to be the first question. In fact, except for the newly created position of chief instructor, current salary dollars are merely reallocated. Using national average teacher salaries at different levels as a reference point,[13] let us say that beginning annual salaries at Mary McCloud Bethune School are $28,000 for associate teachers; $35,000 for teachers; $55,000 for professional teachers; and $20,000 for instructional aides. These are typical salaries for positions at the various levels. The new cost lies in the chief instructor's salary of $80,000. With three chief instructors, the increased annual cost for Mary McCloud Bethune School over a comparable school is $240,000—or $400 per pupil. If we are not to raise local taxes, where will this money come from? Let's look at how a typical school is organized.

In the United States almost half of all public school staff members are not classroom teachers. This proportion is higher than in most other countries. Many of the nonteaching positions—curriculum coordinators, staff developers, teaching coaches, "content coaches," and others—exist at both the school and the administrative levels. They have been cobbled together in an unorganized and unstructured manner to compensate for the weaknesses in the current system—poor teacher training, no mentoring, little or no supervision, ineffective professional development. By folding their responsibilities into its restructured positions, a Millennium School eliminates the need for such ancillary personnel, thereby offsetting the higher salaries for teachers at the upper end of the scale. In addition, the increasing number of retirements anticipated in the next decade will parallel the hiring of less expensive novice teachers. The savings resulting from reallocation of salaries will compensate for the new ranks of teachers envisioned in this model—that is, of course, if the current inadequate salary levels for teachers in this country are maintained. We have to start acknowledging the high social costs of not raising teachers' salaries. "If you think education is expensive," reads the bumper sticker, "think of the alternative." Social scientists have adequately documented the connection between higher levels of education and lower crime rates, something to bear in mind when we consider that 25 percent of the world's incarcerated population resides in this country's prisons and that one of every four housing units being built in the United States is a jail.

The sad fact is that as a nation we resist investment in high-quality teaching, in spite of our collective belief that teachers ought to be making more money. More than 40 percent of Americans believe that teachers are inadequately paid and fully 88 percent say they would favor raising teacher salaries.[14] Yet we continue to reward with both money and prestige those teachers who leave the classroom and to tolerate unskilled and inept teachers who remain. In most European and Asian countries teachers are better prepared in both content and pedagogy before they are allowed to enter the classroom. In many more countries than we care to admit, teachers are more highly respected and better paid than in the United States. When purchasing power is taken into account, seven countries offer teachers higher starting salaries than we do. Nine countries exceed our record in giving teachers at the top of the salary scale more money. Twelve nations invest more in education overall than does the United States.

To go back to the Millennium School, though, instead of costing more, each Millennium School put into operation will actually save tens if not hundreds of thousands of dollars. Because of its collaborative culture and collective responsibility for each student, a Millennium School has a greatly enhanced capacity to serve its students better in far fewer students being held back. Such grade retention is unlikely, so we can deduct a year's worth of schooling from the school district's budget (at the national average cost per pupil of $6,584)[15] for each student who might otherwise have been held back but is propelled into the next grade, thanks to superior teaching. The 3 percent of children held back in the City of Boston adds up to $17 million a year, or 2 percent of the school budget.[16] This financial burden is further increased by necessary "transition programs" to provide individual attention for children who are in danger of being held back, which cost Boston an additional $38 million a year.

Significant savings can be expected when, because of the extra expertise brought to bear by teaching teams, fewer students are identified as "special ed."—a handy category in which to put children who are struggling—the cost of assigning special ed. teachers to those children will go down. Nationally, as teaching expertise declines, special education costs spiral upward. Although special education programs serve only 8 percent of all schoolchildren, they account for about 25 percent of all school expenditures.[17] A Millennium School has the potential to dramatically lower these costs, simply by serving better those children who, in other schools, present too many problems for the inadequately trained teacher to deal with. Too often children are placed on special ed. rosters, even though they have not been diagnosed with a disability, because of a teacher's frustration when a child does not achieve well in a standard classroom. There begins a cycle of failure that becomes only more intractable, and more costly, down the road. Early reading problems, for example, call for early intervention if inappropriate referrals are to be avoided. The interwoven responsibilities inherent in the structure of a Millennium School build in accountability for each student. A single student has a team of teachers assigned to monitor his or her progress, or lack of it, and take prescriptive measures to ensure success.

Then there is the onerous cost of teacher turnover. The U.S. Department of Labor estimates that it costs 33 percent of a new hire's salary to replace an employee. In Texas, 43 percent of new teachers leave after the first three years, and the result in estimated turnover costs is $480 million.[18] As we noted earlier, almost every state in the country suffers high teacher turnover rates. A Millennium School staff enjoys a greatly reduced turnover rate because the conditions that are a major cause of teachers' dissatisfaction (no supervision, no mentoring, no support, job isolation, no opportunities for professional development or career advancement), have been eliminated.

In the end, when all costs are taken into account, better schools with better teaching add up to big savings. *The net result of these integrated reforms is that the cyclical nature of the Trilemma Dysfunction is at last broken.*

How will this happen? Again, as we have said many times, it all comes down to the job of teaching. It is a matter of common sense that good jobs attract the better-qualified candidates. In a Millennium School, teaching is a highly professional enterprise, professionally supervised and supported, and conducted by a cadre of well-paid and highly respected professional educators accountable to one another for achieving success.

When teaching becomes a real profession, with a clearly defined career path that recognizes and rewards merit and achievement, then more academically able people will be drawn into it. When more able people are drawn into the profession, colleges and other teacher preparation programs will be forced, by the power of competition, to improve the quality of their training. When better prepared teachers enter the classroom, the quality of the profession improves and more capable people are eager to enlist. *The circle of dysfunction becomes a spiral of continuous improvement.* Creating a Millennium School will, of course, take time—and that leads to an important question.

What Can We Do *Now*?

We all know that as schools cry out for 2.2 million new teachers, one way or another *someone* will stand at the front of the classroom. We can also predict with a great deal of certainty that a vast majority of those teachers will be even less well qualified for their jobs than the teachers who are entering classrooms today. Without waiting for Millennium Schools to be established throughout the country (admittedly an ambitious task), what can be done right now to minimize the negative impact of so many untrained teachers teaching our children?

Our suggestion is to implement some of the strategies at the core of the Millennium School. In almost any community these steps could be taken:

1. *Restructure the pay scale* so that a new category of senior teachers is created (somewhat analogous to chief instructors or professional teachers in a Millennium School—but not board certified) and given a higher salary. These teachers would be drawn from among the best and most experienced teachers in the system and those who are keen to take on the additional responsibilities of supervising and mentoring novice teachers. Novice teachers would be paid less than they currently are for the first and second years, a condition they will accept in exchange for the superior supervision, training, and experience offered, as well as the opportunity for rapid advancement. Unions should be receptive to this notion, for it would result only in adjusting the pay scale upward or downward, not in a net loss in teachers' salaries.

2. *Set up intensive summer courses* for the new senior teachers, to train them as mentors. Teach for America and some states are already offering intensive summer courses to prepare nontraditional teacher candidates for teaching jobs in September. These novice teachers would be better served if they had fully trained professional teacher mentors at their side. Currently, mentor training, amounting to a few summer workshops, receives short shrift. The role of mentor-teacher in the newly restructured school is critical to its success. Considerable training will be required.

3. *Create teaching teams* of senior teachers, experienced teachers, and novice teachers, who would be responsible for meeting regularly to discuss curriculum, teaching practice, and student progress. Senior teachers would begin to assume responsibility for supervision and curriculum development. Team leaders (who are senior teachers) would report to the principal on student achievement.

4. *Phase out vice-principals, and hire facility managers* to replace

them, freeing the principals to focus on supervision, administrative concerns, and educational leadership, instead of on facility management.

5. *Set up "process boards"* within each elementary school in the system. The boards would be charged with developing an overall strategy and methods for their school's transformation into a Millennium School. This will require, among other things, establishing a relationship with a teachers' college or university willing to create a partnership that would allow their graduate students to participate in a professional development school. Each process board will also gauge the size of its school against the model of a "small school"— meaning no more than six hundred students for each principal—and see to it that a plan is developed to turn each school in the district into a small school.

It is unrealistic to expect that any single model could fit every one of the 105,000 schools in the United States. Each state and local district has its special characteristics, and many kinds of union contracts and collective bargaining agreements are in force. The four central principles undergirding a Millennium School, however, could all be adopted, in some form or other, by any school system in the United States. They are:

- Multi-tiered career paths for teachers
- Teaching in teams instead of in isolation
- Performance-based accountability
- Ongoing professional development for all teachers and principals

This is a flexible strategy that can be implemented in both traditional schools with graded classrooms and more progressive schools with multi-age classrooms. The principles can be tailored to meet the needs of individual schools, districts, and states in reshaping America's schools and the teaching profession.

We are well aware of the hard realities that public education faces.

We acknowledge what is possible and what is impossible. We also understand that although some of what we propose is radical, much is not new. Yet we affirm that every change we propose in the creation of a Millennium School is fully achievable and well within reach in terms of available physical, financial, and human resources.

This is a job that must be done.

Epilogue: E Pluribus Unum

Suddenly, on September 11, 2001, our country came under direct, brutal attack. If many of us felt that our very way of life was being threatened, we were nonetheless heartened by the understanding that, as a democracy, we have the resilience of a unified people to endure and overcome. As a multicultural society, one of the most successful of its kind in history, we draw our strength from many sources. Among our greatest strengths is a shared culture derived from a system of public education that we invented and that serves as a model for the world. It is not by chance that those who seek to build a democratic society begin by adopting a public school system that emulates what we have created.

Today, 40 percent of the people who live in New York City were not born in the United States. That is the same percentage as in 1910. Through what gateway do immigrants and the children of immigrants—like our own children—pass to become Americans? As always, it is the public schools. From generation to generation throughout our history, it has been overwhelmingly the public schools that have disseminated American values to the broad spectrum of society—from the children of Mayflower descendants to the most recent arrivals. Ninety percent of all children in this country attend public schools.

We must not fail to honor and preserve the legacy we have inherited. We must not allow our public schools to become weak and factionalized. We must take the lessons learned in the twentieth century and apply them to the job of rebuilding our schools today.

In the new millennium, we must rise to the challenge of supporting better teaching and learning for our children. Let us remember always that our best investment in a strong America is still the American teacher.

Notes

Introduction

1. John Merrow, *Choosing Excellence: "Good Enough" Schools Are Not Good Enough* (Lanham, Md.: Scarecrow Press, 2001), 83–84.
2. Interview with Ellen Guiney, Boston Plan for Excellence, Boston, Mass., July 2000.

1: Your Children Aren't Getting the Teachers They Deserve

1. D. Haselkorn and L. Harris, *The Essential Profession: American Education at the Crossroads* (Belmont, Mass.: Recruiting New Teachers, 2001), 12.
2. I. Mullin and others, *TIMSS 1999 International Science Report: Findings from IEA's Repeat of the Third International Mathematics and Science Study at the Eighth Grade* (Chestnut Hill, Mass.: International Study Center, Boston College, Lynch School of Education, 2000).
3. A. Eisenkraft, "Rating Science and Math" [electronic version], *Education Week* 20 (22): 4.
4. National Commission on Teaching and America's Future, *What Matters Most: Teaching for America's Future,* report (National Commission on Teaching and America's Future, September 1996).
5. "New Strategies to Curb Teacher Flight from the Classroom Gaining Momentum Nationwide" (Recruiting New Teachers, July 1999, retrieved from http://www.recruitingteachers.org).

6. R. Henke, S. Geis, and J. Giambattista, *Out of the Classroom: 1992–93 College Graduates and Elementary/Secondary School Teaching* (Washington, D.C.: U.S. Department of Education, 1996).

7. National Commission on Excellence in Education, *A Nation at Risk: The Imperative for Educational Reform,* report to the nation and to the secretary of education (Washington, D.C.: U.S. Department of Education, Apr. 1983), 8–9.

8. Albert Shanker, "AFT: Where We Stand: January 12, 1997: A large wooden horse?" (retrieved from http://www.aft.org/stand), 1.

9. National Commission on Excellence in Education, *A Nation at Risk,* 5.

10. Ibid.

11. National Center for Policy Analysis, *Choice in Education: Opportunities for Texas,* Task Force Report No. s148 (Washington, D.C.: National Center for Policy Analysis, 1990, retrieved from http://www.ncpa.org).

12. "Lamar Alexander's Accomplishments" (n.p.: n.d., retrieved from http://www.kent.wednet.edu), 2.

13. R. F. Sexton, "Building Citizen and Parent Support for School Reform: The Pritchard Committee Experience" (Paper presented at the annual meeting of the American Educational Research Association, San Francisco, Calif., April 18–22, 1995).

2: How Teaching Got to Be This Way

1. Data referenced in this chapter are drawn from research by many noted scholars over the past twenty-five years, particularly from David Tyack, *The One Best System* (Cambridge: Harvard University Press, 1976); David Tyack and Larry Cuban, *Tinkering Toward Utopia: A Century of Public School Reform* (Cambridge: Harvard University Press, 1995); Nancy Hoffman, *Woman's "True" Profession: Voices from the History of Teaching* (Old Westbury: Feminist Press, 1981); Lawrence A. Cremin, *American Education: The National Experience, 1783–1876* (New York: Harper & Row, 1980); and Patricia Albjerg Graham, *S.O.S.: Sustain Our Schools* (New York: Hill and Wang, 1992).

2. D. Tyack, *The One Best System: A History of American Urban Education* (Cambridge: Harvard University Press, 1995), 30.

3. Ibid., 45.

4. Ibid., 61.

5. Ibid., 62.

6. C. Beecher, "Remedy for the Wrongs to Women," in Hoffman, *Woman's True Profession*, 48.

7. E. Hickok, "Higher Standards for Teacher Training" [electronic version], *Policy Review* 91 (2), 1998.

8. D. Gitomer, A. Latham, and R. Ziomek, "The Academic Quality of Prospective Teachers: The Impact of Admissions and Licensure Testing" (n.p.: 1999, retrieved from http://www.ets.org).

9. D. Haselkorn and L. Harris, *The Essential Profession: American Education at the Crossroads* (Belmont, Mass.: Recruiting New Teachers, 2001), 21.

10. Maryland State Department of Education, *Parent Handbook for Better Schools* (Baltimore: Maryland State Department of Education, Equity Assurance and Compliance Branch, 2000), 4.

3: Teacher Training

1. The history of teacher education and its current status in the United States have been amply documented. We have drawn on research conducted by many scholars as we prepared this chapter. In particular, we have relied on Merle L. Borrowman, *Teacher Education in America: A Documentary History* (New York: Teachers College Press, 1965); John Goodlad, *Educational Renewal: Better Teachers, Better Schools* (San Francisco: Jossey-Bass, 1994); Jurgen Herbst, *And Sadly Teach: Teacher Education and Professionalization in American Culture* (Madison: University of Wisconsin Press, 1989); and Christopher J. Lucas, *Teacher Education in America: Reform Agendas for the Twenty-first Century* (New York: St. Martin's, 1997).

2. Minutes of the Common Council of Philadelphia—1704–1776, in *July 1, 1750: Benjamin Franklin and the University of Pennsylvania.* Francis Newton Thorpe, ed. (Washington, D.C.: Government Printing Office, 1893).

3. National Center for Educational Statistics, "All Levels of Education," chap. 1 in *1996 Digest of Education Statistics* (NCO-396-133), 12.

4. P. Healy, "6589 Get Degrees at Harvard, Hear Ex-Treasury Aide; Alumnus, 100, Comes by Bus," *Boston Globe,* June 8, 2001, B5.

5. F. T. McCarthy, "Grade-Inflation in Universities," *Economist,* Apr. 14, 2001, 35.

6. G. Mabie, "The Search for Reform: An Interview with Seymour B. Sarason," *Educational Forum* 64 (2): 134–138 (2000).

7. John Merrow, "The Teacher Shortage: Wrong Diagnosis, Phony Cures," *Education Week* 19 (6): 64, 48 (Oct. 6, 1999).

8. Linda Darling-Hammond, as quoted in John Merrow, "A Problem Not of Supply, but of Quality," *Merrow Report,* Dec. 2000–Jan. 2001, 2 (retrieved from http://www.pbs.org).

9. National Commission on Teaching and America's Future, *What Matters Most: Teaching for America's Future* (n.p.: National Commission on Teaching and America's Future, Sept. 1996), 28.

10. D. Hoff, "Arkansas Lowers Hurdles for 'Exceptional' Aspiring Teachers" [electronic version], *Education Week* 20 (32): 20.

11. Georgia Teacher Alternative Preparation Program, "Georgia TAPP" (n.d., retrieved from http://www.teachforgeorgia.org).

12. "Teacher Employment and Subject Expertise" (2001, retrieved from http://www.akrepublicans.org).

13. National Commission on Teaching and America's Future, *What Matters Most,* 15.

14. Ibid.

15. R. M. Ingersoll, "The Problem of Underqualified Teachers in American Secondary Schools," *Educational Researcher* 28 (2): 26–37 (1999).

16. Ibid.

17. National Commission on Teaching and America's Future, *What Matters Most.*

18. Ibid.

19. "Is There a Shortage of Qualified Candidates for Openings in the Principalship?" 1998 study conducted by the Educational Research Service with the assistance of the Gordon S. Black Corporation. National Association of Elementary School Principals website: Principals Online.

20. Statistics on retention rates were derived from the "Statistical History

of Teach for America, 1990–2001," and through e-mail and telephone communications carried out January 15–30, 2002, with Teach for America's public relations department and February 28, 2002, with the manager for alumni operations.

21. L. Bintrim, "Teachers for Today and Tomorrow," *Educational Leadership* 58 (8): 96 (May 2001).

22. Ibid.

23. "VIF Fact Sheet," (n.d., retrieved from http://www.vifprogram.com).

24. K. Sack, "Facing a Teacher Shortage, American Schools Look Overseas," *New York Times,* May 16, 2001, A8.

25. Ibid.

26. J. Hard, "Teacher Candidates Give Low Score to State Test: Pass or Fail, Many Fault Execution and Short Notice," *Boston Globe,* July 10, 1998, B1.

27. Cathy Miles Grant, "Professional Development in a Technological Age: New Definitions, Old Challenges, New Resources" [Technology Infusion and School Change: Perspectives and Practices.] (Cambridge, Mass.: TERC), 72–118.

28. T. Corcoran, *Helping Teachers Teach Well: Transforming Professional Development* (Washington, D.C.: National Governor's Conference, Policy Brief, Consortium for Policy Research in Education, 1995).

29. "Strengthening the Schools: A *Harvard Magazine* Roundtable," *Harvard Magazine* 102 (2): 69 (1999).

30. T. Corcoran, *Helping Teachers,* 3–4.

31. Ibid.

32. The National Board for Professional Teaching Standards was established in 1987 in response to the need for a uniform set of certification standards similar to those in effect in other professions. Certification by the NBPTS ensures a rigorous assessment of a subject, teachers' knowledge, instructional practices, and involvement with colleagues and communities. In a profession that has long resisted the idea, this reform creates differences in teacher status and calls for teaching to become a staged career. Most states support NBPTS certification, and each state has its own array of incentives for teachers who achieve certification. Mississippi, for example, awards an annual bonus of

$6,000, and North Carolina gives those with NBPTS certification an annual 12 percent increase in salary. Not all states are so generous. Kansas provides an annual bonus of $1,000 and Nevada an annual 5 percent increase in salary. Most states also help, to a greater or lesser extent, to fund the $2,300 application fee. In 2001 16,037 teachers were certified in the United States by the NBPTS board.

4: Mamas, Don't Let Your Babies Grow Up to Be Teachers

1. "Mammas, Don't Let Your Babies Grow Up to Be Cowboys," words and music by Ed and Patsy Bruce, recorded by Willie Nelson and Waylon Jennings (1978), recorded by Buddha/Bmg.

2. J. Wilgoren, "Education Study Finds U.S. Falling Short," *New York Times,* June 13, 2001, A26.

3. "Make It Happen: Teach (the Career That Makes a Difference; We Need Teachers)" (n.d., retrieved from http://www.nea.org/students), 2.

4. K. Schneider, and F. Nelson, "Survey and Analysis of Salary Trends, 1997" (April 1998, retrieved from http://www.aft.org).

5. "Lack of Support Makes Teachers Quit" (Mackinac Center for Public Policy, Aug. 15, 1999, retrieved from http://www.educationreport.org).

6. "Nonfatal Teacher Victimization at School: Teacher Reports" (1998, retrieved from http://nces.ed.gov).

7. "Crumbling Conditions Impair Student Learning" (June 15, 2001, retrieved from http://www.weac.org).

8. "Conditions of America's Public School Facilities, 1999" (June 2001, retrieved from http://nces.ed.gov).

9. National Education Association, annual report, *Status of the American Public School Teacher* (National Education Association, 1996).

10. Judie Glave, "Acclaimed Kids' Book Gets Teacher Ousted," *Detroit Free Press,* online, Nov. 25, 1998.

11. The American Association of Colleges for Teacher Education is a national voluntary association of colleges and universities that have undergraduate or graduate programs to prepare professional educators. They describe themselves as "providing leadership for the continuing transformation of professional preparation programs to en-

sure competent and caring educators for all America's children and youth, and the principal professional association for college and university leaders with responsibility for educator preparation" (retrieved from http: //www.aacte.org).

12. D. Tyack and L. Cuban, *Tinkering Toward Utopia: A Century of Public School Reform* (Cambridge: Harvard University Press, 1995).

13. C. Kaestle, *Pillars of the Republic: Common Schools and American Society, 1780–1860* (New York: Hill and Wang, 1983).

14. A. Blumberg and W. Greenfield, *The Effective Principal: Perspectives on School Leadership* (Boston: Allyn and Bacon, 1980).

15. W. Hicks and M. Jameson, *The Elementary School Principal at Work* (Englewood Cliffs: Prentice-Hall, 1957).

16. R. S. Barth, *Run School Run* (Cambridge: Harvard University Press, 1980).

17. W. Hawley and others, "An Outlier Study of School Effectiveness" (Symposium presented at the annual meeting of the American Educational Research Association, Chicago, 1997).

18. A. Blumberg and W. Greenfield, *The Effective Principal.*

19. Educational Research Service, *The Principal, Keystone of a High-Achieving School: Attracting and Keeping the Leaders We Need,* Report for the National Association of Secondary School Principals and the National Association of Elementary School Principals (n.p.: Educational Research Service, 2000).

5: Band-Aids and Boondoggles

1. D. Tyack and L. Cuban, *Tinkering Toward Utopia: A Century of Public School Reform* (Cambridge: Harvard University Press, 1995).

2. Ibid., 66.

3. Ibid., 69–72.

4. J. Heubert and R. Hauser, eds., *High Stakes: Testing for Tracking, Promotion, and Graduation* (Washington, D.C.: National Academy Press, 1999), 13.

5. L. Olson, "Few States Are Now in Line with Bush Testing Plan," *Education Week* 20: 24 (Jan. 31, 2001).

6. G. W. Bush, "Verbatim," *Time,* Jan. 21, 2002, 21.

7. National Association of State Boards of Education, "Cost of President's Testing Mandate Estimated as High as 7 Billion," press release (Alexandria, Va.: National Association of State Boards of Education, Apr. 25, 2001).

8. M. Covington, "The Myth of Intensification," *Educational Researcher* 25: 24–27 (Nov. 1996).

9. C. Snow and J. Jones, "Making a Silk Purse," *Education Week* 20: 60, 41 (Apr. 25, 2001); Jodie Morse, "Test Drive," *Time,* Feb. 4, 2002, 53.

10. Heubert and Hauser, *High Stakes,* 14.

11. D. Henriques and J. Steinberg, "Right Answer, Wrong Score: Test Flaws Take Toll," *New York Times,* May 20, 2001, 1.

12. Lynn Olson, "States Adjust High-Stakes Testing Plans," *Education Week* 20: 1, 18, 19 (Jan. 24, 2001).

13. Ann Bradley, "State of the States: Alaska: Knowles Presses for Delay in State Testing Timeline," *Education Week* 20: 28 (Jan. 17, 2001).

14. Olson, "States Adjust."

15. Alfie Kohn, "Fighting the Tests: A Practical Guide to Rescuing Our Schools," *Phi Delta Kappan* 82 (5): 347–357 (2001).

16. American Educational Research Association, AERA position statement concerning high-stakes testing in Pre-K–12 education (n.d., retrieved from http://www.aera.net).

17. J. Heubert, "High-Stakes Testing: Opportunities and Risks for Students of Color, English-Language Learners, and Students with Disabilities" (National Center on Accessing the General Curriculum, 2000, retrieved from http://www.cast.org/ncac).

18. Olson, "States Adjust," 18.

19. "Congress Asked to Rein in High-Stakes Tests" (FairTest: The National Center for Fair and Open Testing, Spring 2000, retrieved from http://www.fairtest.org).

20. A. Taylor, "Conditions for American Children, Youth, and Families: Are We 'World Class'?" *Educational Researcher* 25: 10–12 (Nov. 1996).

21. Elizabeth Word, "Student/Teacher Achievement Ratio (STAR): Tennessee's K–3 Class Size Study," Final summary report, 1985–1989 (ERIC Document Reproduction Service no. ED320692).

22. J. McRobbie, J. Finn, and P. Harmon, "Class Size Reduction: Lessons

from Experience," Policy brief no. 23 (Washington, D.C.: Office of Educational Research and Improvement, 1998).

23. Ibid.

24. Ibid.

25. E. Hanushek, J. Kain, and S. Rivkin, *Teachers, Schools, and Academic Achievement* (Cambridge, Mass.: National Bureau of Economic Research, 1998).

26. A. Shlaes, "The Next Big Free-Market Thing," *Wall Street Journal,* July 9, 1998.

27. B. Jackson, "School Choice: It's About Children, Stupid!" (retrieved from http://www.goodschools.com).

28. A. Molnar and C. Achilles, "Voucher and Class-Size Research," *Education Week* 20: 64 (Oct. 25, 2000).

29. P. McEwan, "The Potential Impact of Large-Scale Voucher Programs," *Review of Educational Research* 70: 103–49 (Summer 2000).

30. "An Evaluation: Milwaukee Parental Choice Program" (State of Wisconsin, 1999–2000 Joint Legislative Committee, Legislative Audit Bureau, Feb. 2000).

31. American Federation of Teachers, "Vouchers vs. Small Class Size" (American Federation of Teachers, retrieved from http://www.aft.org).

32. D. Myers and others, "School Choice in New York City After Two Years: An Evaluation of the School Choice Scholarship Program" (Program on Education Policy and Governance, John F. Kennedy School of Government, Harvard University, Aug. 2000), 40–44.

33. M. Carnoy, "Do School Vouchers Improve Student Performance?" *American Prospect* 12 (1): 1 (Jan. 1–15, 2001).

34. "School Vouchers: The Wrong Choice for Public Education" (n.d., retrieved from http://www.adl.org).

35. Voucher programs in the United States can be either privately funded (through scholarships) or publicly funded (through taxes). Children First America puts the number of children attending school under private voucher programs at 100,000—see M. Ladner, "Just Doing It 5," *Executive Summary* 5 (2): 2 (July 2001). Terry M. Moe, professor of political science at Stanford University and an author of *Private*

Vouchers (Hoover Institution Press, 1995), and Tom Loveless, director of the Brown Center on Education Policy at the Brookings Institution, both estimate the number of students attending schools on publicly funded vouchers to be fewer than 15,000.

36. "Making Schools Work Better for All Children: Charter School Highlights and Statistics" (2000, retrieved from http://edreform.com).

37. "Texas Open-Enrollment Charter Schools: Third-Year Evaluation" (March 2000, retrieved from http://www.tea.state.tx.us).

38. National Education Association, "Charter Schools: A Look at Accountability," 5 (Apr. 1998, retrieved from http://www.nea.org).

39. D. Harrington-Lueker, "When a Charter Fails," *School Administrator,* Aug. 1997.

40. T. Good and J. Braden, "Charter Schools: Another Reform Failure or a Worthwhile Investment?" *Phi Delta Kappan* 81: 745–750 (June 2000).

41. Ibid.

42. L. Weiner, "Standardization's Stifling Impact," *Education Week* 20: 29, 33 (Feb. 28, 2001).

43. Sprout Group, "Edison Schools: Backing an Entrepreneur with a Big Idea" (2001, retrieved from http://www.sproutgroup.com).

44. S. Greenberger, "For-Profit School Firm Falls Short on Reforms," *Boston Globe,* May 13, 2001.

45. B. Milner, "For-Profit Firm on the Ropes," *Rethinking Schools* (Spring 2000).

46. G. Geboski, "State IG: Charter School Has $ Trouble," *Somerville* [Mass.] *Community News,* May–June 2000.

47. American Federation of Teachers, Department of Research, "Survey and Analysis of Teacher Salary Trends" (1999, retrieved from http://www.aft.org).

48. American Association for Employment in Education (2001, retrieved from http://www.ub-careers.buffalo.edu).

49. Data derived from telephone conversations with officials of the Westchester County Department of Education on May 15 and 17, 2001.

50. "How to Find and Keep Teachers" (n.d., retrieved from http://www.recruitingteachers.org).

51. H. Kaufman, "Down the Out Staircase," *Boston Globe,* Aug. 19, 2001, L12.

52. "The Urban Teacher Challenge: Teacher Demand and Supply in the Great City Schools," report of the Urban Teacher Collaborative (Belmont, Mass.: Recruiting New Teachers, Jan. 2000).

53. Recruiting New Teachers, "Learning the Ropes: Urban Teacher Induction Programs and Practices in the United States," 1999 (retrieved from http://www.recruitingteachers.org).

54. National Education Association, "News and Publications: Creating a Teacher Mentoring Program" (NEA Foundation for the Improvement of Education, 1999, retrieved from http://www.nea.org).

55. W. Wilms and R. Chapleau, "The Illusion of Paying Teachers for Student Performance," *Education Week* 19: 48, 34 (Nov. 11, 1999).

56. D. Tyack and L. Cuban, *Tinkering Toward Utopia,* 130.

57. "Pay-for-Performance: An Issue Brief for Business Leaders" (Business Roundtable and National Alliance of Business, July 27, 2000, retrieved from http://www.brt.org).

58. National Commission on Teaching and America's Future, *What Matters Most: Teaching for America's Future* (New York: National Commission on Teaching and America's Future, 1996), 5.

59. S. Russell, "The Role of Curriculum in Teacher Development," in *Reflecting on Our Work: NSF Teacher Enhancement in K–6,* S. N. Friel and G. W. Bright, eds., 247–254 (Lanham, Md.: University Press of America, 1997).

60. K. Manzo, "Ignoring Advisory Panel, California Adopts Skills-Based Math Textbooks," *Education Week* 20 (Jan. 17, 2001).

61. "Grading the Graders" (Online NewsHour: Testing Teachers, Sept. 15, 1998, retrieved from http://www.pbs.org).

62. M. Winerip, "Homework Bound," *New York Times,* Jan 3, 1999, Education Life Supplement.

63. R. Ratnesar, "The Homework Ate My Family," *Time,* Jan. 25, 1999, 56, citing the Survey Research Center of the University of Michigan Institute for Social Research.

64. National Center for Education Statistics, *The Condition of Education, 1996* (Washington, D.C.: National Center for Education Statistics,

National Assessment of Educational Progress, Office of Educational Research and Improvement, U.S. Dept. of Education, 1996).

65. G. Chaika, "Help! Homework Is Wrecking My Home Life!" [electronic version], *Education World* Aug. 8, 2000, 1.

66. "Homework: Time to Turn It In?" (Apr. 1999, retrieved from http://www.nea.org).

67. E. Kralovec and J. Buell, *The End of Homework: How Homework Disrupts Families, Overburdens Children, and Limits Learning* (Boston: Beacon Press, 2000).

68. G. Stager, "Questioning Homework's Worth" (Jan. 26, 2001, retrieved from http://www.educatorsportal.com).

69. J. Cloud and J. Morse, "Home Sweet School," *Time,* Aug. 27, 2001, 158.

70. U.S. Department of Education, *Homeschooling in the United States* (Washington, D.C.: U.S. Department of Education, 1999).

71. J. Cloud, "Home Sweet School," 49.

72. "Learning Round the Kitchen Table," *Economist* 347: 28 (June 6, 1998).

73. C. Cardiff, "The Seduction of Homeschooling Families" (retrieved from http://www.fee.org).

74. D. Kirkpatrick, "Teacher Unions and School Reform in Pennsylvania," (1998, retrieved from http://www.schoolreport.com).

75. Impact of the Unions, "The 30th Annual Phi Delta Kappa/Gallup Poll of the Public's Attitude Toward the Public Schools," *Phi Delta Kappa International,* Sept. 1998 (online version, retrieved from http://www.pdkintl.org/kappan/kp9809-a.htm).

76. C. Haar and M. Lieberman, "NEA/AFT Membership: The Critical Issues" (1997, retrieved from http://www.educationpolicy.org).

77. *American Educator* (Spring–Summer 1997, Special Issue), 30.

78. American Federation of Teachers, *Building a Profession: Strengthening Teacher Preparation and Induction*—Report of the K–16 Teacher Education Task Force (Washington, D.C.: American Federation of Teachers, Apr. 2000).

79. "ER&D and Professional Development," *American Teacher,* Sept. 2000, Special Report no. 2.

80. E. Hertling, "Peer Review of Teachers" [electronic version] ED429343 1999-05-00 *ERIC Digest,* no. 126.

81. "How Teachers' Unions Are Working with Districts to Improve Schools," *Challenge Journal* (Spring 2001).

82. Ibid., 7.

83. A. Odden, "Rewarding Expertise" [electronic version], *Education Matters* (Spring 2001).

84. John F. Kennedy, as quoted by Megan Deshoyers, First Annual Community Forum on Historical Records, Massachusetts Foundation for the Humanities, 1998 Advocating Massachusetts History Forum (retrieved from http://www.cs.umb.edu/jfklibrary).

6: The Millennium School

1. J. D. Saphier, *Bonfires and Magic Bullets: Making Teaching a True Profession, the Step Without Which Other Reforms Will Neither Take nor Endure* (Carlisle, Mass.: Research for Better Teaching, 1995).

2. National Commission on Teaching & America's Future, *What Matters Most*.

3. H. Stevenson, and J. Stigler, *The Learning Gap* (New York: Summit Books, 1991).

4. The idea of grand rounds, based on the model of medical school training, is not new. In 1987 the two of us, along with Wheelock College colleague Karen Worth, founded one of the first professional development schools in the country. The Learning/Teaching Collaborative (L/TC) was a collaboration between Boston and Brookline, Massachusetts, public schools and Wheelock and Simmons Colleges. As part of this PDS (which, in an evolved form, still exists), several innovations were experimented with, implemented, and then adopted elsewhere when L/TC became a model for other PDS endeavors. It was in our minds to implement grand rounds at L/TC and we put in place a version of the grand rounds idea we have since modified and fine-tuned for the Millennium School. We began grand rounds with an emphasis on the training of teacher interns, who signed up to participate in rounds three times a month. A classroom teacher in one of the schools conducted a research study of grand rounds that revealed what a powerful effect grand rounds was having on the participating teachers as well. Teachers reported that their own practice was being positively affected in ways they had not anticipated, and

they wanted grand rounds to expand so that more of them could participate more fully. That is why, in a Millennium School, the practice of grand rounds includes all teachers and all teaching interns. It was our belief then, and it still is, that transforming teaching from a private to a public act is critical to education reform. Today, grand rounds is being considered for inclusion in a few professional development schools around the country. South Knoll Elementary School in Bryan, Texas, for example is in a PDS partnership with Texas A&M University, which operates under NCATE standards. At South Knoll, preservice teachers watch as an experienced teacher delivers a prepared lesson. They take notes and gather later to exchange observations and critique what they have observed. This is an excellent start, but our experience strongly suggests that fuller participation by all teachers is necessary if the teaching culture of isolation is to be substantially altered. As a strategy to transform teaching from a private to a public act, grand rounds could play an important role in education reform.

5. Alternative professional time, another idea that was implemented successfully in the Learning/Teaching Collaborative, was designed to meet teachers' expressed need to supplement their classroom work with wider professional growth opportunities. In a school environment that supports the classroom teacher with well-trained teaching interns, APT provides classroom teachers with one day a week (six hours) away from teaching duties to assume alternative roles. It also provides opportunities for teachers to learn new skills and gain expertise in areas of particular interest. Instituting APT helps create a culture in which professional development is no longer restricted to afternoon workshops with topics mandated by a central office and no longer perceived by teachers as "deficit training." Also, APT work emerges from the interests of individual teachers. During their APT, some teachers conduct research to improve their own teaching or to test the assumptions of educational theory and practice. Others take on the primary responsibility of teaching graduate student interns and designing appropriate curricula that connect the theories and research studied at the college with actual classroom practice. Some teachers

develop, pilot, implement, and evaluate new curricula as part of town-wide curriculum initiatives or develop curricula with local educational consulting firms.

6. Recent initiatives have encouraged research by teachers at their own schools, as school districts and teachers themselves look for more meaningful forms of professional development. Most teachers are still expected to attend after-school workshops designed elsewhere in the school hierarchy, but there is a move to encourage teachers to initiate their own professional development through research. Teacher-researchers, often working in groups, define their own research questions and collect and analyze data with the express purpose of improving teaching and learning in their classrooms.

7. "National Board for Professional Teaching Standards" (2001, retrieved from http://www.nbpts.org).

8. R. S. Barth, *Run School Run*, 173.

9. A. Rotherham, "When It Comes to School Size, Smaller Is Better," [electronic version], *Education Week* 18 (24): 76 (Feb. 24, 1999); Center for Education Reform, "Who's in Charge: The Education Establishment," chap. 4 in *The School Reform Handbook* (Washington, D.C.: Center for Education Reform, 1995).

10. M. Scherer, "Why Think Small?" *Educational Leadership*, Feb. 2002, 5.

11. D. Meier, *The Power of Their Ideas* (Boston: Beacon Press, 1995), 107.

12. Despite compelling evidence that smaller is better, large schools continue to be built; however, as communities come to recognize and understand the benefits of small schools, new opportunities arise for reconfiguring large buildings into schools-within-a-school. In 1992, Naomi Booker, principal of Philadelphia's Clymer Elementary School, divided her nine hundred students into three "learning communities" with spectacular results. Since then, more than six hundred such communities have been created in Philadelphia's elementary and middle schools, prompted in part by the requirements of the Children Achieving Challenge, a public-private partnership funded by Walter Annenberg's grant of $50 million to public education. The Bill & Melinda Gates Foundation and the Carnegie Corporation of New York are

supporting the creation of about a thousand new small schools, some of them to be converted to schools-within-schools. In Chicago, the Small Schools Workshop at the University of Illinois is working with seventy-two elementary and high schools to create schools-within-schools. In New York City, the Center for Collaborative Education (CCE) and New Visions for Public Schools are working collaboratively to create small schools to serve as models for districts around the country. The Northwest Regional Education Laboratory is collaborating with the California Institute on Human Services at Sonoma State University to provide training and technical assistance for schools that receive Smaller Learning Communities grants from the U.S. Department of Education. The small-schools movement, begun as a reaction against the ills perpetuated by monstrously large high schools, is gaining momentum in middle and elementary schools as well, and not only in large urban school districts. It is an idea whose time has come, and any school in the United States wishing to create a small school has many successful models to emulate.

13. National Center for Education Statistics, *Digest of Education Statistics, 2000* (Washington, D.C.: U.S. Department of Education, Office of Educational Research and Improvement, 2000), Table 77, p. 85.

14. D. Haselkorn and L. Harris, *The Essential Profession: American Education at the Crossroads* (Belmont, Mass.: Recruiting New Teachers, 2001).

15. National Center for Education Statistics, *Digest of Education Statistics, 2000,* Table 170, p. 192.

16. Boston Public Schools, Fiscal Year 2002 Budget (Boston: Boston Public Schools, Mar. 28, 2001), 111. The budget is based on per-pupil spending of $7,596.

17. Kate Zernike, "Special Education Debate Shifts from Money to New Ideas" (May 11, 2001, retrieved from http://www.nytimes.com).

18. Texas State Board for Education Certification, "The Cost of Teacher Turnover" (Austin, Tex.: Texas Center for Educational Research, Nov. 2000), 3.

Bibliography

Banner, J. M., Jr., and Cannon, H. C. *The Elements of Learning.* New Haven: Yale University Press, 1999.

Barth, R. S. *Run School Run.* Cambridge: Harvard University Press, 1980.

Barth, R. S. *Improving Schools from Within.* San Francisco: Jossey-Bass, 1990.

"A Better Balance: Standards, Tests, and the Tools to Succeed: Quality Counts 2001." An *Education Week*/Pew Charitable Trusts report on education in the 50 states. *Education Week,* January 11, 2001.

Biklen, S. K. *School Work: Gender and the Cultural Construction of Teaching.* New York: Teachers College Press, 1995.

Blumberg, A., and Greenfield, W. *The Effective Principal: Perspectives on School Leadership.* Boston: Allyn and Bacon, 1980.

Boles, K., and Troen, V. "Teacher Leaders and Power: Achieving School Reform from the Classroom." In *Every Teacher as Leader: Realizing the Potential of Teacher Leadership,* Moller, G., and Katzenmeyer, M., eds. San Francisco: Jossey-Bass, 1996.

Boles, K., and Troen, V. "How the Emergence of Teacher Leadership Helped Build a Professional Development School." In *Making Professional Development Schools Work: Politics, Practice, and Policy,* Levine, M., and Trachtman, R., eds. New York: Teachers College Press, 1997.

Borrowman, M. L., ed. *The Liberal and Technical in Teacher Education.* New York: Bureau of Publications, Teachers College, Columbia University, 1956.

Borrowman, M. L., ed. *Teacher Education in America: A Documentary History.* New York: Teachers College Press, 1965.

California Commission on the Teaching Profession. *Who Will Teach Our Children? A Strategy for Improving California's Schools.* Sacramento, Calif.: California Commission on the Teaching Profession, 1985.

Callahan, R. E. *Education and the Cult of Efficiency: A Study of the Social Forces That Have Shaped the Administration of Public Schools.* Chicago: University of Chicago Press, 1962.

Cohen, J., and Rogers, J., eds. *Will Standards Save Public Education?* Boston: Beacon Press, 2000.

Cremin, L. A. *The American Common School: An Historic Conception.* New York: Bureau of Publications, Teachers College, Columbia University, 1951.

Cremin, L. A. *American Education: The National Experience, 1783–1876.* New York: Harper & Row, Harper Colophon Books, 1980.

Cuban, L. *How Teachers Taught: Constancy and Change in American Classrooms, 1880–1990.* 2d ed. New York: Teachers College Press, 1993.

Darling-Hammond, L., ed. *Professional Development Schools: Schools for Developing a Profession.* New York: Teachers College Press, 1994.

Darling-Hammond, L., and Goodwin, A. Lin. "Progress Toward Professionalism in Teaching." In *Challenges and Achievements of American Education: 1993 Yearbook of the Association for Supervision and Curriculum Development,* Cawelti, G., ed. Alexandria, Va.: Association for Supervision and Curriculum Development, 1993.

Delpit, L. *Other People's Children: Cultural Conflict in the Classroom.* New York: New Press, 1995.

Dewey, J. *The School and Society.* Rev. ed. Chicago: University of Chicago Press, 1915.

Doud, J. L., and Keller, E. P. *The K–8 Principal in 1998.* Alexandria, Va.: National Association of Elementary School Principals, 1998.

Elmore, R. *Building a New Structure for School Leadership.* Washington, D.C.: Albert Shanker Institute, 2000.

Finn, C. E., Jr., and Rebarber, T., eds. *Education Reform in the '90s.* New York: Macmillan, 1992.

Fullan, M. *Change Forces: Probing the Depths of Educational Reform.* Bristol, Pa.: Falmer Press, Taylor & Francis, 1993.

Fullan, M. *What's Worth Fighting for in the Principalship?* New York: Teachers College Press, 1997.

Glasser, W. *The Quality School: Managing Students Without Coercion.* New York: Harper & Row, Perennial Library, 1990.

Goodlad, J. *Educational Renewal: Better Teachers, Better Schools.* San Francisco: Jossey-Bass, 1994.

Graham, P. A. *S.O.S.: Sustain Our Schools.* New York: Hill and Wang, 1992.

Gross, M. L. *The Conspiracy of Ignorance: The Failure of American Public Schools.* New York: HarperCollins, 1999.

Hanushek, E.; Benson, C. S.; Freeman, R. B.; Jamison, D. T.; Levin, H. M.; Maynard, R. A.; Murnane, R. J.; Rivkin, S. G.; Sabot, R. H.; Solmon, L. C.; Summers, A. A.; Welch, F.; and Wolfe, B. L. *Making Schools Work: Improving Performance and Controlling Costs.* Washington, D.C.: Brookings Institution, 1994.

Haselkorn, D., and Harris, L. *The Essential Profession: American Education at the Crossroads.* Belmont, Mass.: Recruiting New Teachers, 2001.

Hasenstab, J. K., and Wilson, C. Corcoran. *Training the Teacher as Champion.* Nevada City, Calif.: Performance Learning Systems, 1998.

Herbst, J. *And Sadly Teach: Teacher Education and Professionalization in American Culture.* Madison: University of Wisconsin Press, 1989.

Heubert, J. P., and Hauser, R. M., eds. *High Stakes: Testing for Tracking, Promotion, and Graduation.* Washington, D.C.: National Academy Press, 1999.

Hicks, W., and Jameson, M. *The Elementary School Principal at Work.* Englewood Cliffs, N.J.: Prentice-Hall, 1957.

Hoffman, N. *Woman's "True" Profession: Voices from the History of Teaching.* Old Westbury, N.Y.: Feminist Press, 1981.

Hoffman, N. E.; Reed, W. M.; and Rosenbluth, G. S. *Lessons from Restructuring Experiences: Stories of Change in Professional Development Schools.* Albany: State University of New York Press, 1997.

Ingersoll, R. M. *Teacher Turnover and Teacher Shortages: An Organizational Analysis. American Educational Research Journal* 38 (3): 499–534 (2001).

Johnson, S. M. *Teacher Unions in Schools.* Philadelphia: Temple University Press, 1984.

Johnston, M.; Brosnan, P.; Cramer, D.; and Dove, T., eds. *Collaborative Reform and Other Improbable Dreams: The Challenges of Professional Development Schools.* Albany: State University of New York Press, 2000.

Kaestle, C. E. *Pillars of the Republic: Common Schools and American Society, 1780–1860.* New York: Hill and Wang, 1983.

Kimbrough, R. B., and Burkett, C. W. *The Principalship: Concepts and Practices.* Englewood Cliffs, N.J.: Prentice Hall, 1990.

Kozol, J. *Savage Inequalities: Children in America's Schools.* New York: Crown, 1991.

Kralovec, E., and Buell, J. *The End of Homework: How Homework Disrupts Families, Overburdens Children, and Limits Learning.* Boston: Beacon Press, 2000.

Kramer, R. *Ed School Follies: The Miseducation of America's Teachers.* New York: Free Press, 1991.

Kwiatkowski, M. *Debating Alternative Teacher Certification: A Trial by Achievement.* Claremont, Calif.: Tomas Rivera Policy Institute, 1998.

Lieberman, A., ed. *Rethinking School Improvement.* New York: Teachers College Press, 1986.

Lieberman, A., ed. *Building a Professional Culture in Schools.* New York: Teachers College Press, 1988.

Livingston, C., and Castle, S., eds. *Teachers and Research in Action.* Washington, D.C.: NEA Professional Library, 1989.

Logan, J. *Teaching Stories.* Saint Paul: Minnesota Inclusiveness Program, 1993.

Lortie, D. C. *Schoolteacher: A Sociological Study.* Chicago: University of Chicago Press, 1975.

Lucas, C. J. *Teacher Education in America: Reform Agendas for the Twenty-first Century.* New York: St. Martin's Press, 1997.

Meier, D. *The Power of Their Ideas: Lessons for America from a Small School in Harlem.* Boston: Beacon Press, 1995.

Merrow, J. *Choosing Excellence: "Good Enough" Schools Are Not Good Enough.* Lanham, Md.: Scarecrow Press, 2001.

Milken, L. *A Matter of Quality: A Strategy for Assuring the High Caliber of America's Teachers.* Santa Monica, Calif.: Milken Family Foundation, 1999.

Murnane, R. J., and Levy, F. *Teaching the New Basic Skills: Principles for Educating Children to Thrive in a Changing Economy.* New York: Free Press, Martin Kessler Books, 1996.

Nanus, B. *Visionary Leadership: Creating a Compelling Sense of Direction for Your Organization.* San Francisco: Jossey-Bass, 1992.

Reid, R. L., ed. *Battleground: The Autobiography of Margaret A. Haley.* Urbana: University of Illinois Press, 1982.

Saphier, J. D. *Bonfires and Magic Bullets: Making Teaching a True Profession, the Step Without which other Reforms Will Neither Take nor Endure.* Carlisle, Mass.: Research for Better Teaching, 1995.

Sarason, S. B. *The Creation of Settings and the Future Societies.* San Francisco: Jossey-Bass, 1972.

Sarason, S. B. *The Predictable Failure of Educational Reform: Can We Change Course Before It's Too Late?* San Francisco: Jossey-Bass, 1990.

Sarason, S. B. *You Are Thinking of Teaching? Opportunities, Problems, Realities.* San Francisco: Jossey-Bass, 1993.

Sarason, S. B. *Charter Schools: Another Flawed Educational Reform?* New York: Teachers College Press, 1998.

Sarason, S. B. *Political Leadership and Educational Failure.* San Francisco: Jossey-Bass, 1998.

Sarason, S. B. *Teaching as a Performing Art.* New York: Teachers College Press, 1999.

Shulman, L., and Sykes, G., eds. *Handbook of Teaching and Policy.* New York: Longman, 1983.

Traub, J. *Better by Design? A Consumer's Guide to Schoolwide Reform.* Washington, D.C.: Thomas B. Ford Foundation, 1999.

Troen, V., and Boles, K. "Two Teachers Examine the Power of Teacher Leadership." In *Teachers as Leaders: Perspectives on the Professional Development of Teachers.* Walling, D. R., ed. Bloomington, Ind.: Phi Delta Kappa Educational Foundation, 1994.

Troen, V., and Boles, K. "Leadership from the Classroom: Women Teachers as a Key to School Reform." In *Women Leading in Education,* Dunlap, D. M., and Schmuck, P. A., eds. Albany: State University of New York Press, 1995.

Tyack, D. B. *The One Best System: A History of American Urban Education.* Cambridge: Harvard University Press, 1974.

Tyack, D., and Cuban, L. *Tinkering Toward Utopia: A Century of Public School Reform.* Cambridge: Harvard University Press, 1995.

U.S. Department of Education. *Promising Practices: New Ways to Improve Teacher Quality.* Washington, D.C.: U.S. Department of Education, 1988.

Warren, D., ed. *American Teachers: Histories of a Profession at Work.* New York: Macmillan, 1989.

Whitford, B. L., and Jones, K., eds. *Accountability, Assessment, and Teacher Commitment: Lessons from Kentucky's Reform Efforts.* Albany: State University of New York Press, 2000.

Index